VICKI TenHAKEN

LESSONS FROM CENTURY CLUB COMPANIES
Managing for Long-Term Success

Spinner Press
Division of Sales Aerobics for Engineers®, LLC
3588 Plymouth Road, #264
Ann Arbor, MI 48105
www.spinnerpress.com

Lessons from Century Club Companies:
Managing for Long-Term Success
© 2016 Vicki TenHaken

ISBN: 978-0-9848986-0-2
Library of Congress Control Number: 2015960586

Printed in the United States of America
Cover and internal design: Anne Sutton
Editing: Clark Malcolm
First Printing: 2016

Legal Considerations

Spinner Press
Division of Sales Aerobics for Engineers®, LLC
3588 Plymouth Road, #264
Ann Arbor, MI 48105
www.spinnerpress.com

Acknowledgements

I am profoundly indebted to my research partner, Makoto Kanda. This book is the result of his work, and without Mako's inspiration and backing I would not have embarked on this journey.

Both my children worked with me at crucial stages in the research that forms the basis for this book: Alison Sale made significant contributions to building the database and Nicholas Meshkin worked tenaciously to obtain the survey returns needed for statistical analysis. I am deeply appreciative of their interest and involvement in my work.

Several Hope College student researchers worked on this project over the years and Katelyn Rumsey deserves special recognition for her contributions.

And a big thank you goes to Clark Malcolm, without whose editing and encouragement this book would have remained an unpublished manuscript.

For the leaders at Herman Miller, Inc. who exemplified the principles described in this book and shaped my views about business long before this research began.

And for the many leaders of companies, both old and new, who recognize that relationships matter most—in business as in life. These leaders know that a business can do well while doing good.

Contents

PREFACE

After more than 25 years in business, the last decade as an executive in a $2 billion international company, I began a second career as a college professor at the start of a new millennium. I looked forward to trying to encourage future business leaders consider the role business plays—or might play—in building our society. I wanted to help them understand how, by becoming competent and caring business professionals, they could enable the companies they join (or start) be positive contributors to society as a whole. My interactions with students and the teaching role of college professor still inspire me. However, the work of a tenured professor requires scholarship in addition to teaching. I needed a research agenda.

My first paper for an academic conference resembled those of many other former executives: leadership lessons I had learned from the real world. That paper, titled "Everyday Leaders" (I later discovered even the title was not appropriate for an academic paper; it is way too short), received more attention and positive response than I could have hoped for, and I was encouraged. But having built my case for the importance of good, everyday management, I didn't have much more to say about that topic and found myself a little at sea as to how to proceed to build a real scholarly agenda.

So it was my good fortune to be asked to lead our school's Japan May Term in 2004. Ever since backpacking through Europe between my junior and senior years in college, I have loved traveling to other countries and learning about different cultures. Though at the time I knew relatively little about Japan, I readily volunteered to be the faculty leader of the program.

Hope College, where I still teach, has had a decades-long relationship with Meiji Gakuin University in Tokyo. We celebrated 50 years of exchange programs in 2015.

This relationship enables our May Term in Japan to be much more than travel and touring, and we spent most of the month in Tokyo taking in lectures from various MGU professors. One such lecture was given by economics professor Makoto Kanda, who presented his work studying *shinise*, ancient and honored Japanese companies, or "old companies of long standing." I was fascinated. The common characteristics of these organizations in many ways echoed my own beliefs about how businesses should be run. Here potentially was proof that my ideas weren't unreasonably idealistic, even though many of the practices Mako described weren't usually taught in business schools.

Several of the oldest known continuously-operating companies in the world are Japanese. Seven were founded prior to the year 1,000. The size of companies in the database of Japanese firms over 100 years old clearly proves that firms do not have to grow large to survive. In fact most *shinise* are small- to medium-sized, private (often family-owned) businesses. This revelation especially impressed me, considering how ingrained the maxim of "grow or die" has become in modern management theory.

After returning from Japan, I couldn't stop thinking about Mako's presentation. Several questions came to mind: How unusual is it for a company to live to be 100 years old? If it is rare, how have some companies managed to beat the odds? Are there any secrets to corporate longevity we could learn by studying the management practices of the old companies? Since Japan has such a concentration of old companies, how culturally specific are these behaviors? Would old companies in the United States exhibit similar practices?

I had found my research agenda. And even better, Mako agreed to work with me.

INTRODUCTION

Most firms do not survive as long as they could. Various studies indicate the average life span of companies today is 12 to 15 years. And the average age of the largest companies is shrinking. The life span of companies on the Standard & Poors 500 Index has decreased by more than 50 years in the last century. The average age was 67 years in the 1920s but just 15 years in 2013. Experts have suggested the natural life span of a corporation could be as long as 200 to 300 years.

Forty-four organizations throughout the world now belong to the Henokiens Association. Membership requires longevity (the minimum age to qualify for membership is 200 years), permanence (the family must be owner or majority shareholder of the company, and the founding family must still manage the company or be a member of the board), and performance (the company must be in good financial health). Even in a country as young as the United States, well over 600 companies have survived for more than 100 years. They have become what I like to call "Century Club" companies. But these firms represent less than one-half of one percent of companies operating in the U.S. today. When evaluating company performance in terms of years of existence versus possible longevity, we can't help but conclude that most firms do not live up to their potential.

A premise of this book is that a fundamental objective of any organization, though often unstated, is survival. As Arie de Geus explains in the prologue to his book *The Living Company*, "Like all organisms, the living company exists primarily for its own survival and improvement, to fulfill its potential and to become as great as it can be." Similarly, profits are the means to survive and thrive for companies. As business guru Peter Drucker pointed out, profits are the cost of the future. They are necessary for survival, but they may not be the ultimate goal of a business. Profits are fuel for a company's engine; they aren't the destination.

Businesses, he says, exist for much more than to produce profits for shareholders, just as humans exist for more than our work. We all want to survive and thrive, and working at a job is a means to that end. Similarly, profits are the means to survive and thrive for companies.

Why be concerned about corporate longevity? Gary Hamel, whom the *Wall Street Journal* has ranked as the world's most influential business thinker and *Fortune* magazine has called the world's leading expert on business strategy, wrote in his WSJ blog that when companies die prematurely, it is to the detriment of society at large. He points out that time enables complexity and organizations grow and prosper by turning simple ideas into complex systems. The process of turning inspiration into value takes time, proceeding as it does through iterative cycles of experiment-learn-select-codify. If poor executive decisions prematurely interrupt this process, a society may lose the benefit of the original idea, as well as others it may engender along the way. This isn't an argument to insulate a company from failure, he says, but rather a reason to "imbue organizations with the capacity to dynamically adjust their strategies as they pursue a long-term mission."

Echoing Hamel, de Geus points out that corporate failure often means the collapse of an entire ecosystem. The damage caused by the premature death of a company "is not merely a matter of shifts in the Fortune 500 roster; work lives, communities, and economies are all affected, even devastated, by premature corporate deaths." Biologists suggest that no living species could survive such a large gap between potential life expectancy and actual average age. De Geus additionally observes: "Few other types of institutions—churches, hospitals, or universities, for instance—seem to have the abysmal demographics of the corporate life form." De Geus concludes that companies die prematurely because managers focus exclusively on economic activity, forgetting that an organization's ultimate goal should be to become a community of humans.

In the words of Ian Davis, former managing director of the multi-national management consulting firm McKinsey & Company, "in a very real sense, survival is the ultimate performance measure."

What enables some companies to defy the odds and continue operating for a century or more while most others succumb to an early death? Well over 95 percent of all businesses are small- and medium-sized enterprises and privately-owned, according to the U.S. Census Bureau. Previous research on corporate longevity has dealt with large, mostly publicly-owned companies using very small sample sizes (Collins & Porras, 1994; Pascale, 1990; Hall, 1997; de Geus, 1999; Grossman & Jennings, 2002; Stadler, 2007; Kwee, 2009). For this reason, the research I embarked on with my Japanese partner Makoto Kanda focused on small- and medium-sized, privately-owned firms. We wanted our research to be useful to a majority of companies today desiring to thrive for the long run. We wanted the practices we revealed to be relevant.

The longevity practices of Century Club companies described in this book result from ten years of research in both Japan and the United States. Professor Kanda's and my work began with case studies of several old companies in Japan and the United States from which we built a theoretical longevity model. This model identifies and examines the practices the case study companies said led to their survival for over a century. To test our model, we administered a survey of 125 questions about the model's key factors to 90 Japanese companies over 100 years old. Their responses confirmed that Century Club companies believed the practices described in our model are indeed important factors in their longevity. Then the survey was sent to all 7,000 companies in the Chuo Ward of Tokyo, Japan, both old and young, to see if the behaviors described in our longevity model were unique to Century Club companies. A number of statistically significant practices of old companies emerged.

When hearing the results of this research at academic conferences, people most often ask Mako and me whether these behaviors are unique to Japan. Was our longevity model really describing Japanese businesses and therefore not relevant to organizations in the United States or other economies? After taking several years to construct a database of U.S. companies over 100 years old, we were able to test our framework for its relevance in the United States. We translated our survey into English and sent it to U.S. companies over 100 years old. Not only did the results confirm the validity of our longevity model in the United States, the U.S. companies told us that many of the significant Century Club practices are even more important to them than to their Japanese counterparts.

Though the practices Mako and I identified exist in companies in business for over a century and many are not practiced by younger companies, implementing these practices alone cannot guarantee a company's survival for the long run. Too many economic and social factors, not to mention the results of poor leadership, affect the life spans of businesses. Also, the statistical significance of these practices does not mean that all Century Club companies employ all the practices we uncovered.

Be assured that the longevity practices described in this book are not just my personal recommendations for better business management. They are based on objective research. These practices come from literally centuries of experience in long-lived companies in Japan and the

United States. I am happy to admit that they do coincide with my beliefs about how business should be conducted, which probably explains why I became so interested in this research in the first place and have had such fun putting this book together.

It did not surprise me that the behaviors described in our longevity model are now showing up in 21st century management theories: "stakeholder theory" (obtaining a competitive advantage through the development of close-knit ties with a broad range of internal and external constituencies); and "shared value" (the policies and operating practices that enhance the competitiveness of a company while simultaneously advancing the economic and social conditions in the communities in which it operates), which has been called the next evolution of capitalism[1]. Century Club companies have thrived for over 100 years by successfully practicing a way of doing business that creates shared value and enables their own survival long before such ideas came to be described as the evolution of American capitalism.

When I began preparing for one of my research presentations, I realized every job I've had—from bank teller to employee relations specialist to executive vice president of strategy—was with a company over 100 years old. Perhaps my own work experience helped form my beliefs about the role companies should play in society. In any case, I am happy to say research confirms that the practices benefitting all stakeholders also enable an individual firm's survival for the long term.

---

[1] "Creating Shared Value: Redefining Capitalism and the Role of the Corporation in Society," January 2011 *Harvard Business Review*, by Michael E. Porter, a leading authority on competitive strategy at Harvard Business School, and Mark R. Kramer, Kennedy School at Harvard University.

THE LONGEVITY MODEL

Based on in-depth interviews and subsequent surveys of companies in business for more than one century, five factors emerged that these companies believe contribute significantly to their long-term survival. Leaders of the Century Club companies say these practices build loyalty to their firms, in particular with customers and employees. They also believe their approach to doing business is difficult for competitors to imitate and helps their firms to thrive. Here are brief descriptions of the five components of our longevity model. Later chapters will describe these factors in more detail along with the unique practices employed by enduring enterprises. The leaders of the case study Century Club companies were adamant that all these factors must be implemented together to sustain a firm for the long run: together they form a mutually reinforcing web of sustainable business practices.

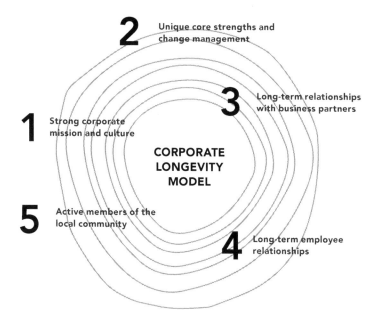

2 Unique core strengths and change management

3 Long-term relationships with business partners

1 Strong corporate mission and culture

CORPORATE LONGEVITY MODEL

5 Active members of the local community

4 Long-term employee relationships

FACTOR 1: Strong corporate mission and culture

The existence and deliberate preservation of certain values and beliefs that form a strong corporate culture are a key survival factor among Century Club companies. Most have values developed by a founder and passed on through the generations. Certain lessons, warnings, and exhortations are described and communicated in these teachings. Though the style and content differs from company to company (for instance, not all firms have written mission or values statements), current leaders consistently affirm the importance of their corporate credo as a primary factor in the success of their businesses. These traditional values and beliefs underlie the fundamental culture of the company and both enhance employee identification with the business and attract and retain customers.

Present leaders of Century Club companies see themselves as stewards or custodians of the business and feel an obligation to manage the firm in a way that both honors the past and ensures its survival into the future. This deliberate focus on continuity, rather than making a name for themselves, results in real differences in the way old companies are managed.

FACTOR 2: Unique core strengths and change management

The existence and protection of a particular technical specialty or core competency is a second factor the Century Club companies say is important to their longevity. These company "secrets" or special methodologies make the organization and what it offers unique. Further, the enduring enterprises say the ongoing development of their special capability is also necessary. The image of old companies is often that they stick to tradition and resist change. Nothing could be further from the truth. The reality is that they adapt and successfully implement change to survive the many challenges encountered over the centuries. Long-term survival comes from continuous efforts to change while protecting and building on core strengths—a delicate balance between tradition and change.

FACTOR 3: Long-term relationships with business partners

Relationships are at the core of how the Century Club companies operate. These firms regard the maintenance of long-term relationships with customers and the development of their suppliers from generation to generation as crucial to their own success. These companies truly believe they cannot maintain their success over decades and even centuries without such a web of interdependence. The emphasis on relationships with business partners goes beyond mere economic transactions or the exchange of goods or services for financial gain. The resulting close-knit, mutually-supportive relationships heighten the company's ability to weather challenges as well as to learn and adapt over time.

FACTOR 4: Long-term employee relationships

The development and maintenance of long-term relationships with employees is another keystone factor in the longevity framework. Many employees become lifelong, loyal members of the organization and often describe their relationship with the company as being part of a family. One of the important employee practices used by the old companies is the development of leaders from within, using a deliberate process for leadership succession. A majority of these firms have already identified their next leader.

FACTOR 5: Active members of the local community

Because the old companies see themselves as an integral part of a web of relationships (often connected to their family history and reputation), the development of relationships within the local community—both commercial and social—become as important as the development of relationships with business partners. Century Club companies participate actively in their local communities, promoting them and developing local networks for mutual learning and benefit. The Century Club companies believe their businesses greatly benefit from having a good standing in their community. They also say that a community's good reputation helps their business, so enduring enterprises invest time and resources in projects that develop and sustain their communities.

Some of these longevity factors have been described by others, such as Collins and Porras in their book *Built to Last*, Arie de Geus in *The Living Company*, and Christian Stadler in *Enduring Success*. However, these studies describe very large, publicly-owned firms. Our longevity model draws most heavily on small- to medium-sized, privately-owned firms. (Though some of the companies researched were publicly traded, they tended to be closely held with family members often involved in the company.) The last factor, community involvement, is unique to this study and, we believe, a key factor in the ability of these old companies to thrive for over a century. As the Henokiens Association says about their member companies in business for over 200 years, the specific characteristics of these old companies' backgrounds and the common values that unite them constitute a message of hope for all businesses, especially those with a desire to form the economic and social fabric of the future.

Strong Corporate Mission and Culture

W.C. Bradley Co. (1885)

The W.C. Bradley Co. could only survive and thrive because of very strong values shared by everyone. It also survives because the owners were always willing to take a long-term view, often foregoing attractive short-term opportunities when they did not fit with their vision and long-term goals. These core values based on integrity and stewardship have served the company well over the years and we continue to live by them.[2]

Carrollton Bank (1877)

My great-great grandfather was a founding partner of the bank. He was the first of an unbroken string of five generations to lead Carrollton Bank, and he had some pretty sound ideas. So sound, in fact, that they're still around for you to take advantage of today. Throughout these many decades, through wars, depressions and even the constant change in today's banking industry, there remains—and will always remain—one constant: the solid values, passed down from generation to generation, which govern how we treat our customers.

Menasha Corporation (1852)

Menasha Corporation has cultivated a culture of possibilities, a spirit fueled partly by 160 years of family values and partly by a tireless desire to deliver value to customers. It is evident every working day whether interacting with one another, our customers or our stakeholders.

---

[2] All quotations come from company websites except as indicated.

The existence and deliberate transmission of values and beliefs that form a strong corporate culture is considered a key survival factor by the Century Club companies. In many these values were developed by the founder and passed on through the generations. Like the idea of a "relatively fixed core ideology," identified by Collins and Porras in their book *Built to Last*, these values and beliefs function as the fundamental business guidelines for the firm and provide the core ideas with which members of the company can identify. Most Century Club companies have strong oral traditions represented in sayings such as, "When the store is open there's always a Fabiano on the floor." Or "The customer is always #1—that means you call them by their name." Or "We don't play pricing games—we offer a good, first deal." Or "Strangers are only friends we haven't met yet." Some are simply common sayings like "We follow the Golden Rule" or "Be fair and honest."

A corporate credo or mission statement, however, is not a characteristic limited to Century Club companies. Eighty-eight percent of the old companies surveyed had some sort of mission statement; 85 percent of young firms also did. There are, however, some significant differences in the content of the old companies' mission statements and in how they use this sense of purpose and values to manage the company and shape corporate culture.

Century Club companies emphasize relationships with their business partners in their credos and tend to include statements about the special technologies or skills that make their company unique. The old firms showed the most differentiation from other firms in the ways they actually live up to their mission statements. They score higher on every aspect of credo utilization, strongly emphasizing actually managing according to the credo. In other words, the old companies really live their mission statements, which go beyond words developed for their website or following the fad for mission statements as a popular management practice. As the current owners of Burdine's Five and Dime (1908) in Harrisville, West Virginia put it:

> *The store's philosophy remains just the same as it was when K.C. first opened its doors a century ago: treat each customer special while striving to maintain a friendly shopping experience. Today, every customer is greeted warmly, with our employees understanding that treating others with civility is more important than making a sale.*

The Century Club companies are also more intentional about sharing their credo with others, teaching it to employees, as well as discussing it with customers and other business partners. The special values of the founders or other significant historical leaders of the businesses and their beliefs about how business should be conducted form a strong culture in the old companies, one that employees identify with—it simply becomes "the way things are done around here." Woe to any manager who tries to cut corners or act contrary to the established values. Employees in Century Club companies act as a sort of corporate antibody that overcomes potential infection from people who violate cultural or behavioral norms.

Leaders of enduring enterprises expressed a strong desire to carry their mission and culture into the future. Clearly the corporate values describe how the business was managed in the past and for today, but also form a framework for continuity into the future. As a current partner in the 185-year-old law firm Curtis, Mallet-Prevost, Colt & Mosle (1830) says:

> *Everyone sees themselves as trusted advisors to their clients, rather than big-shot attorneys, which is similar to how lawyers thought of themselves centuries ago. The firm isn't trying to make the most money or become the largest company. There's a commitment to continue what has come before.*

The importance of corporate culture is also seen in the way the old firms regard their brand identity. Century Club companies pay great attention to the representation and protection of their company or brand name. They make sure there is consistency in the way the brand is used and want the brand to be prominent in their products, facilities, written materials, and wherever the company or its major offerings are represented. Name and reputation mean everything to these companies, and they guard them carefully.

Though cultures in the Century Club companies are very strong, the specifics of the cultures vary widely. There is, however, one common cultural aspect of the old companies: a conservative approach to managing finances. These firms are very reluctant to go into debt as a way of funding their business. (One leader recounted with glee how he had ignored the advice from a Lehman Brothers consultant that his firm was under-leveraged and they should take on more debt.) The Century Club companies also place more importance on profitability than growth. These practices are likely the reason a large majority of companies over 100 years old are small- to medium-sized businesses. As sixth-generation owner Kevin Hancock of Hancock Lumber Co. (1848) put it:

> *I'm not surprised there is no correlation between being large and long-term survival. In fact, if anything, perhaps the opposite is true. Most of the companies in our industry I have seen go out of business did so during periods of unsustainable growth and overreaching.*

Managing with conservative financial practices, Century Club companies tend to be very profitable. In 2004, the average net profit for old Japanese companies studied was twice that of the average profitability for all Japanese companies according to the Japan Ministry of Finance. Christian Stadler's 2007 study of old European firms showed profit margins over time were more than 10 percent higher than margins in younger comparison firms. Well-established, unique products (see factor #2) obviously contribute to the profitability of these companies, but

Century Club companies also operate at a level of leanness and efficiency that is a distinguishing factor. Frugality in running the business enables the company to set aside money in prosperous times to help weather the lean years. This approach to financial management also means money is available to internally fund new opportunities when they arise, thus avoiding external sources of financing, or having to convince others of the value of an initiative. With cash reserves, the Century Club companies are able to respond quickly to take advantage of opportunities they see, as well as invest in innovations others may not see as worth the risk of going into debt to finance.

This approach to financial management is well described by Arie de Geus in *The Living Company*: "Long-lived companies were conservative in financing. They were frugal and did not risk their capital gratuitously. Having money in hand gave them flexibility and independence of action. They could pursue options that their competitors could not. They could grasp opportunities without first having to convince third-party financiers of their attractiveness."

The benefit of this approach to managing finances is evident in the 125th anniversary video posted on the website of brokerage and investment banking firm Stifel (1890):

> *While many firms faltered, our fiscal responsibility allowed us to flourish during the financial crisis of 2008. Not only did Stifel not require a government bailout, we were able to capitalize on opportunities and position ourselves for continued success.*

A fundamental objective of the Century Club firms is survival, and staying financially sound is a means to this end. But for these company leaders making a profit is not an end in itself: it is the means to sustain their business. Stone carver Nick Benson of The John Stevens Shop (1705) in Newport, Rhode Island, says the business has survived for over 300 years for two reasons. He is not concerned about making big bucks, and he cares deeply about his work. "We don't care about the money as much as we care about the product. I'm inspired by the legacy I've received."

This is the profit paradox of Century Club companies: though they don't define the purpose or mission of their company as making money, they are very profitable. In their book *Built to Last*, Collins and Porras also described this view of profits on the part of long-lived firms: "Profitability is a necessary condition for existence and a means to more important ends, but it is not the end it itself . . . . Profit is like oxygen, food, water, and blood for the body; they are not the point of life, but without them, there is not life." As Max De Pree of Herman Miller, Inc. (1905) says, profit is the result of doing well what they do as a company, not their goal.

Century Club companies talk passionately about the purpose of their business. Whether it is to enhance human life (pharmaceutical company), create great places to live and work (furniture manufacturer), or provide a bit of sunshine to every customer's day (candy store), the purpose of these old companies is clear and meaningful. They talk about their purpose all the time with employees, with customers, with suppliers, their local community, academic researchers, and pretty much anyone who will listen. They love what they do, and it shows.

Unique Core Strengths and Change Management

McIlhenny Company (1868)

Edmund McIlhenny secured a patent in 1870 and TABASCO® Sauce began its journey to set the culinary world on fire. Over 140 years later, TABASCO® Sauce is made much the same way on Avery Island, Louisiana. The current Chairman of the Board and CEO is the seventh McIlhenny in a chain of direct descendants who have strived to preserve the legacy and traditions of the company's creator.

Sawyer Bentwood (1801)

At Sawyer Bentwood, we use a one-of-a-kind technique for steam bending wood to ensure quality and consistency. We manufacture specialized hardwood furniture components including edge bands, table aprons, chair backs, rocker runners, slats and bow backs using our unique method for steam bending wood. Our proprietary system ensures uniformity, quality & consistency.

Hunter Fan Company (1886)

Sure, we invented the ceiling fan—but every day, we find new ways to perfect it. That's our challenge and our passion. Why? Because a ceiling fan is something special. It's more than a mere appliance or fixture—it's a piece of fine furniture that's also incredibly functional. What other home furnishing can maximize comfort, energy efficiency and aesthetics in every room?

Whether talking literally about a secret sauce, such as McIlhenny Company's Tabasco® sauce, or using the term metaphorically to refer to a particular technical specialty or core competency, most of the companies that have survived for over 100 years attribute their success partly to the accumulation over time of some specialized knowledge, skills, or technology. The Century Club companies believe their "secrets" or special methodologies make the organization and their offerings unique. Such a differentiation strategy sets them apart from the competition and makes what they do difficult for others to imitate, thus giving the company a sustainable competitive advantage over time. This approach to business, which offers differentiation from the competition and is difficult for others to imitate, falls in line with academic and author J.B. Barney's "resource-based view" of competitive advantage.

The beliefs held by the old companies that they have unique core competencies, that their products or services are difficult to copy, and that their offerings have a strong appeal other than price do not significantly differ from those of a majority of younger firms. However, the old firms are more likely to build on their special skills or technologies in every aspect of their business, including the fine details of their offering, how they train and educate new employees, how they work with suppliers, and how they convey their uniqueness to customers as part of the sales process.

Another area where management of strengths is unique among Century Club companies lies in how they strengthen their core competencies over time. Though the old companies say some things should not change—product quality, raw and processed materials, production and sales methodologies—they are constantly working to improve their operations as well as develop and improve their core competencies. As W.C. Bradley (1885) puts it:

> *A company that is not moving forward will lose in this very competitive world. For that, we strive continuously to be creative and innovative in what we offer. To remain successful, we continuously need to learn new ways and be willing to adapt and adjust.*

Members of the corporate Century Club know what is unique in their DNA, and they cherish, protect, and build upon it.

Just one example of this ongoing process of innovation building on core strengths is the Jelly Belly Candy Company (1898):

> *The second generation of the Goelitz candy making family specialized in making Candy Corn and buttercreams. Though sugar rationing during World War II limited candy production, they continued to experiment with new items and introduced Mint Wafers during this time. In the 1960s, third and fourth generation descendants of founder Gustav Goelitz started making candies such as tangerine slices, spice drops—and jelly beans. An innovation was made in 1965 when they infused their Mini Jelly Beans with flavor in the center. In 1973 they introduced the classic Chocolate Dutch Mints. Then in 1976 the first eight flavors of the eponymous mini jelly bean, Jelly Belly, were introduced. The rest, as they say, is history with more Jelly Belly flavors constantly being developed and pushing the flavor horizon: savory flavors, sours, beans inspired by the Harry Potter series, a "performance" bean that provides carb replenishment, and the world's first chocolate covered jelly beans, and more. And, yes, they still make Candy Corn and Chocolate Dutch Mints.*

Century Club companies are not dinosaurs. They would not have survived world wars, economic depressions, globalization, changing social and cultural mores, and quantum leaps in technology that created whole new industries (and obsoleted others) without innovation and change. As the CEO of 130-year-old Cromwell Architects (1885) says, "flexibility is what has allowed us to survive, change, and grow." Enduring enterprises have learned to respond to social and economic change without losing themselves and their uniqueness. As Peter Drucker reminds us in *The Essential Drucker*, it is not necessary for a company to grow bigger, but it is necessary for a company to constantly grow better.

The way Century Club companies go about changing seems to make the difference. Collins & Porras described this unique approach to change in *Built to Last*: "Visionary companies display a powerful drive for progress that enables them to change and adapt without compromising their cherished core ideas."

Old companies tend to take their time when implementing major change. Because they want to carefully balance the old and the new, they feel they must first affirm their traditional past before altering what no longer works or embarking on something entirely new. This balance of tradition and innovation is a carefully choreographed process designed to honor the past while recognizing the need to change in order to survive. Even though approaching change this way takes longer, it appears to be a significant factor in successful adaptation over time. Century Club companies take the time to first honor what was good about the past, and then to educate all constituencies (including employees, suppliers, and customers) about the need for change, as well as offering the training and development necessary for participants to update skills and technologies to change along with the company. Thus Century Cub companies are able to move forward while keeping their support systems intact. As a college professor, I could not help but notice that the change management practices used by the old companies follow the principles of successful change implementation taught in business courses today. It is rewarding to see what we teach confirmed by successful, real-world businesses.

Century Club companies have precious histories and a heritage they protect at all costs. At the same time, they do not stubbornly observe their traditions without challenge. Their ability to change by first affirming their traditional past and then altering what is necessary—the balance of tradition and innovation—enables their long lives. Here is a story about how two organizations (which are real, but whose names have been withheld) navigated through difficult business transitions. The approaches used to implement necessary changes exemplify what a difference it makes when a leader follows the longevity principle of balancing tradition with change.

Both companies in this story had very strong cultures that were employee-focused, one might even say paternalistic. Both firms had loyal employees, many with several decades of service and multiple family members working for the company. Both companies were going through a leadership transition at a time of difficult industry dynamics and faced a dismal business forecast. Company A brought in a well-respected leader who was president of another company; Company B (a Century Club company) promoted a member of their executive team to become CEO. Each new CEO believed his company had become too inwardly-focused and that change was needed if the company was to succeed in the new competitive realities facing their industry. The main difference lies in how the two leaders navigated their company through the changes they thought necessary.

The first action of the new CEO of Company A was to fire or retire most of the existing leadership team. Many of the people he brought in to replace them were managers who had worked for him in his previous firm. His instructions to them were to change the culture of the company from what he saw as one of employee entitlement to one of operational efficiency. As declining sales drove the need to make deep budget cuts, he used it as an opportunity to remove many long-term employees he felt were barriers to change. He also made major cuts in the firm's R&D investments, though this had always been one of the company's core strengths. The people who remained in the company weren't quite sure how to be effective in this new reality. They became demoralized and lamented the loss of the company as they knew it. The new CEO never was able to energize the company in a new direction. He decided to take an early retirement and the Board hired a new CEO.

Company B's new CEO also believed major changes needed to take place. He gathered information on the current industry reality and projections for the future and built the case for change, personally making most of the presentations to managers and employees. Once people understood the reality of the company's situation, they were asked for their ideas and help. The CEO promised the company would continue to invest in developing new and innovative products, but they also needed to find a way for operations to become more efficient if they were to survive. Employee involvement was a long-standing tradition in the company, and the new CEO used the culture of participation both to identify and to implement the changes. This company also needed to reduce the size of its workforce because of drastically deteriorating industry conditions, but did so in such a way that it still ended up on *Fortune*'s list of "Best Companies to Work For." Today this company continues to introduce disruptive products and it is also one of Toyota Production System's prize pupils.

The point of this story: Don't walk away from your past when change needs to take place, build on it. Change is absolutely necessary to survive over the long term, but how you change makes a difference. A company's culture and core competencies can change and evolve. They are the building blocks to be used to make changes in Century

Club companies. Changing through building on your company's core competencies and unique technologies rather than abandoning them may make take longer but will be far more effective in the long run. In an interview with McKinsey's Rik Kirkland, Heineken NV (1864) executive board chairman and CEO Jean-François van Boxmeer discusses managing for the long term against a backdrop of corporate tradition and changing consumer and societal demands:

> *In balancing the short, medium, and long term, I think you have to spot the opportunities and map them. . . But take a look at 20 or 30 years, and then come back. That's what you have to do when you lead a business which is 150 years old and still planning to go another 150 years.*

Long-Term Relationships with Business Partners

E.C. Barton & Co. (1885)

Early on, Eugene Barton learned his father's philosophy on business: 'I've spent my life insisting that my employees follow the same rule—treat your customers courteously, give them quality merchandise and stand behind everything you sell. Buy quality, buy satisfaction has always been our motto.' It is better not to sell a customer at all, than to sell him once.

Gordon Food Service (1897)

We believe in the power of good food—to bring people together and make moments special. Every product, every order, and every decision we make is inspired by the people on the other side of the plate. Today's Gordon Food Service family is united in our commitment to serve our customers today and help them grow tomorrow.

Herman Miller, Inc. (1905)

With each other and with our customers, designers, dealers, suppliers, and contractors, good relationships are the basis of our networks around the world.

Bixler's Jewelers (1785)

We attribute our success as jewelers over 225 years to a painstaking dedication to our customers. The word 'customers' actually seems so rude and impersonal to us, since we have always felt more like a big extended family and special friends. And, thanks to our longstanding relationship with the Fischler Diamond Company in Antwerp, Belgium, we are able to offer you better diamonds for less money.

The approach to managing change used by Century Club companies described in the previous chapter grows out of the importance they place on maintaining their relationships. They understand that their companies are parts of large, interdependent systems. These companies know they cannot control everything around them and that they must depend on a complex web of people and organizations beyond the walls of their firm. When pursuing internal change, Century Club companies patiently work with their external partners, so that no one is left behind once the change is implemented. The systemic effect of this approach is to reinforce the loyalty of customers and develop the dedication of other business partners to the success of the company. Thus the old companies are more often able to survive upheavals in their industry, advances in technology, and other environmental changes outside their control.

Since Century Club companies believe they cannot maintain success without the cooperation of others, they put a premium on actions that will retain their suppliers and customers from generation to generation. They regard working with vendors to develop the capabilities needed to continue to supply their own organization as an obligation. Continuing to provide long-term customers with the products and services they desire is seen as a responsibility. Responding to new needs or problems identified by customers results in learning and development that helps ensure the firm's survival. Incorporating new technologies developed by suppliers and other business partners helps keep the Century Club companies relevant.

The relationships with business partners that result in mutual learning are examples of the behaviors proposed by Peter Senge in his description of "learning organizations." Learning organizations facilitate competitive advantage through employee engagement in the customer experience and collaboration with key business partners, which ultimately boosts business performance. And as former CEO of General Electric (1879) Jack Welch states, "An organization's ability to learn and translate that learning into action is the ultimate competitive advantage."

Because these old companies view relationships with their business partners as something more than economic transactions or the trading of goods and services for financial gain, they are willing to share technologies and ideas that other companies would consider company-confidential. The willingness to learn from all transaction partners is seen by the old companies as an important factor in their long-term survival. Century Club companies truly believe part of the reason for their success comes from their long and deep relationships with customers and suppliers. This emphasis on long-term relationships leads to a kind of symbiosis with their business partners. Close-knit, mutually-supportive relationships help the old companies and their partners learn and adapt over time, often resulting in longevity for all involved.

Old companies are significantly more likely than younger firms to emphasize their corporate values and product story when working with customers, and they also make more of an effort to see that their products are used in the best way. Further, old companies work hard to gain an understanding of key customers, using customer service and after-sales services as a way to build long-term relationships and to learn from them. Often the old companies define their purpose in terms of helping customers accomplish their purpose, such as this statement from DWS Printing (1865): "We are the last step in the visions of a lot of passionate people. . . . Our purpose is to help actualize your vision, to help tell your story, and to become a part of your legacy." And the Herman Miller, Inc. (1905) mission: "Inspiring designs to help people do great things."

Older firms are also significantly more likely to share information with their suppliers, including communications regarding company production methods, sales processes, products, and services, as well as information about the company's customers and markets. Century Club companies are more likely than younger firms to feel it is important to understand the corporate policies and business strategies of their suppliers. They tend to treat suppliers as if they are an extension of their own company, and over time this closeness becomes a true partnership. Such trust built up over generations becomes a great competitive advantage to the entire network.

This emphasis on long-term relationships does not prevent the old companies from seeking out new business partners. In our research, old companies place even more importance on developing new customers than younger ones do. However, the old companies truly believe they cannot maintain their success for a long period of time without the help of their business partners. When customers and suppliers become trusted business partners, both parties are willing to share information and do favors for each other that don't necessarily result in any readily apparent financial gain. The willingness to share information, technologies, and ideas becomes a two-way street, resulting in mutual learning, mutual success, and enduring trust.

This longevity factor of long-term relationships with customers applies across industries. When I first started researching 100-year-old companies, I thought there was a preponderance of retail organizations, and it made sense that building good customer relations was an important factor in ensuring repeat business. But after building a comprehensive database of 100-year-old U.S. companies across industries, we found that retail firms do not represent a higher percentage of the Century

Club companies than in the general business population. Century Club companies scored extremely high on issues of building long-term customer relationships regardless of industry. It may seem obvious that old companies are more likely to emphasize their corporate history, culture, and product "story" when working with customers. But it goes beyond the selling. The old companies are significantly more likely than younger firms to make every effort to see that their products are used in the best way. They also build their relationships with customers through after-sales services, responding quickly to customer complaints and using customer service as an important opportunity to talk with and connect to customers (not just to fix the immediate problem). This interest in how customers use the company's products or services often leads to learning opportunities and future changes and improvements. Such close relationships with customers and suppliers are used as learning opportunities to provide insights and information. They help old companies to survive upheavals in their industry, advances in technology, and other environmental and social changes that often leave their competitors behind.

When I attended IBM's 100th anniversary celebration as a guest speaker, I sat in the back of the room for the opening keynote address. One of IBM's corporate leaders talked about the company culture that enabled them to survive for the last century. One item she mentioned was the long-term relationships with customers, which led to mutual learning and success. Without any prompting—or knowledge of who I was and what I did—the gentleman sitting next to me leaned over and said, "Our company has been an IBM customer for 80 years, and I can tell you what she's saying is absolutely true. They work with us all the time on problems we have and help us find ways to address them."

Swedish investor Marcus Wallenberg says: "Established firms have a huge natural advantage in the marketplace because of their strong customer and supplier bases." Former McKinsey managing director Ian Davis in his 2014 reflections on corporate longevity in the *McKinsey Quarterly* says that older companies "relentlessly focus on their customers, and not just on their performance with customers but also on understanding what their best and most innovative customers are doing." And the older companies "engage their key suppliers to solve problems and identify opportunities, so that these activities also become key sources of insight." By viewing their relationship with business partners as something more than the exchange of goods and services for financial gain, Century Club companies build supportive networks that reap great benefits in the long run and help ensure not only survival, but success.

Long-Term Employee Relationships

Hickok & Boardman Insurance Group (1821)

While some of us bear the names of the founders of this company, we are built on many individuals and families who reach out to our clients every day. We are very proud of our team, and to this day we have multiple generations of family members who have worked for this company over the years, each passing down our tradition of superior service.

Cranston Print Works (1807)

Cranston Print Works was one of the first companies to become employee-owned when the Employee Stock Ownership Plan (ESOP) concept was conceived in the 1970s. Over the years, our employees have become increasingly passionate about their jobs and their Company, as anyone who is an owner of his own business can appreciate. The individual employee owners directly benefit when their company succeeds, thus no one has a stronger interest in the quality of their products and the total satisfaction of their customers than the employee owners.

The Collins Companies (1855)

One of the things that make this company different can be summed up in the word humanitarian. A compassion for other people. The generations of people who have worked for this company are family. They stay year after year, generation after generation, and I have to believe it's because of the way they're treated. (Lee Diane Collins Vest, 4th generation, Collins board member)

Relationships lie at the heart of Century Club companies. The development and maintenance of long-term relationships with employees is no exception. Many employees of these companies become lifelong, loyal members of the organization and often compare their relationship with the company to being part of a family. Often multiple members of the same literal family work for the company "family," and some talk about their parents and grandparents also working for the firm.

Building relationships with employees so they stay with the firm for a long time is consistently described as a key longevity success factor by 100-year-old companies. For instance, General Mills (1866), even with over 16,000 employees, manages to maintain a turnover rate of just three percent. More than half its workers have been on the job for 10 years; nearly 3,500 for more than 20. Employment with retail building supply store chain E.C. Barton & Company (1885) is about stability: More than 24 percent of their "partners" have been with the company for 10 or more years, and almost 12 percent have been there for more than 20 years. Grain milling company C.H. Guenther & Sons, Inc. (1851) makes their commitment to employees clear in their statement of values, which includes "fostering long-term relationships." Referring to employees as "associates," they commit to providing competitive pay and benefits along with the opportunity for continuous learning, challenge, and growth.

Whether talking about efforts to retain employees or investments in their training and development, century-old companies clearly believe keeping employees for the long-term is a differentiating factor. Though this is a very important element in Century Club companies' longevity, it does not appear to be statistically significant when compared to philosophies reported by younger companies. When responding to our longevity model survey, young companies also indicated it was important to them to build long-term relationships with employees. Though young companies put slightly less importance on practices relating to employee retention, it was not a statistically significant difference. The only practice significantly differentiating old from young companies is the effort old companies take to teach employees about company history and tradition, perhaps because younger companies don't yet have much history or many traditions.

One explanation for the lack of significant difference between old and young companies' self-reported behavior toward employees could be that many companies now realize retaining well-trained employees is of great benefit to their business. As Bill Marriott, CEO for 40 years, says of Marriott International (founded 1927, so not quite 100 years old), "A seasoned workforce does a better job—and they cost you less money." Another possible explanation is that younger companies intend to operate this way but have not yet been tested during tough times. Will they use workforce cutbacks as a primary method of responding to business downturns, or will they actually keep employees on the payroll during tough times the way the older companies have? Do young companies simply talk a good game regarding the importance of employees? In any case, companies surviving for over 100 years clearly believe in and support practices that build long-term relationships with employees.

There is plenty of evidence that many of the best companies, whether young or old, have realized that treating employees well and avoiding turnover is just good business. In the 2015 *Fortune* issue highlighting great places to work, Geoff Colvin says:

> *Here's the simple secret of every great place to work: It's personal. It's relationship-based, not transaction-based. Astoundingly, many employers still don't get that, though it was the central insight of Robert Levering and Milton Moskowitz when they assembled the first 100 Best Companies to Work for list in the early 1908s. 'The key to creating a great workplace,' they said, 'was the building of high-quality relationships in the workplace.'*

Colvin goes on to say that human capital is growing more valuable every day in every business. As this trend has been going on for decades and just keeps growing, companies will continue to gain a competitive advantage by attracting and keeping the most valuable workers. This approach to employee relations, however, is not a "trend" the old companies have latched onto. It is ingrained in the way they have done business for a century or more. And in case you harbor any doubts that such practices can be profitable, companies seen as good places to work by employees really do outperform other companies as investments. Since 1998 the 100 Best Companies have outperformed the S&P 500 index by a ratio of nearly 2 to 1.

Century Club companies invest in the training and development of their employees. They are especially deliberate about teaching employees the history of their company in addition to the technologies and skills employees will need to keep the company successful into the future. Because of this investment made in their employees, the old companies make every effort to retain them. The connection between employee training investments and long-term employment is well documented by Stanford University professor Jeffrey Pfeffer in his description of the human resource practices of successful companies, in publications such as *The Human Equation: Building Profits by Putting People First and Seven Practices of Successful Organizations*. Labor economists would say it doesn't make sense to spend company resources on employee development if you don't expect them to stay with the firm to see the payoff for that investment.

Many of the old companies reported keeping employees on the payroll even when they didn't have enough work to keep them busy at their regular tasks. They might do this by having employees temporarily engage in maintenance work or development activities. Some firms even "lent out" their employees to non-profit organizations during slow business times. When business picked up again, these firms didn't have to worry about recruiting, screening, selecting, and training new workers, all of which takes time and resources. The old companies choose to invest their resources in employee retention rather than replacement. Such employee retention practices build great loyalty to the company on the part of employees and enhance company performance. This is an area where we easily see the interconnection of the longevity factors. If the company hadn't been financially conservative during the good years, it wouldn't have the resources to keep paying employees during a business downturn and thus be able to quickly respond to the upturn when it comes.

Since so many of the old companies are small, they report that they can't always compete with the pay and benefits offered by larger firms, so they find other ways to make employment with their company attractive. This may be through flexible schedules or other (often informal) family-friendly practices, along with profit-sharing or bonuses when business is good. Some have gone so far as to have employee stock ownership plans—even privately-owned firms have set up such plans. As Colvin said in the previously mentioned *Fortune* article, "The real key is interpersonal relationships: employees are more engaged where relationships thrive, [especially] in the smallest companies."

Old companies believe long-term employees bring a wealth of "institutional memory" to issues and opportunities that arise. After years with the company, employees identify very closely with the firm and its goals. Many of the Century Club companies engage in some type of profit-sharing, employee ownership, or participatory management practices. Even without any type of formal ownership in the company, employees in these companies develop an ownership attitude—it's their company. The resulting integration of personal and organization goals and objectives has a major impact on the company's success. Employees conduct their work and use company resources as if they were their own. This sense of employees and the company being partners in making a company successful extends to union relationships. Bill Kennedy, third generation president of family-owned asphalt and paving company Rock Road Companies (1913), said in a 2015 interview with *New York Times Magazine*, "There's this misguided myth that unions and management don't get along. The unions are my partner."

The identification with the company on the part of employees is a powerful advantage for a business, but it also makes it very difficult for executives brought in from outside the company to succeed. Employees take a "wait and see" attitude toward a newly hired executive. Will this new leader take the time to learn the company patterns of behavior, or come in with the attitude that she or he has a better way? (illustrated in the change management story on page 27) It can take a very long time for an old company to accept an outsider who joins the company as an executive and it takes a special person to be willing to come in at that level and pay the dues necessary to be successful as an outsider. As a result, most old companies only bring in external candidates to fill executive positions as a last resort.

It is thus not hard to see why one of the important distinguishing characteristics of the 100-year-old companies is the development of leaders from within. Most Century Club companies say they have in place a systematic process for leadership succession. They like future leaders to first have experience in other companies, but they must then work from the ground up, including hands-on experience in their company's operations. Once leaders thoroughly understand the business and have built their own personal networks of relationships both inside and outside the company, then they are expected to think for themselves rather than blindly following tradition.

One Century Club company's CEO said that the development of his successor is his most important task, and he wasn't anywhere close to retirement age at the time he made this statement. The majority of 100-year-old companies report they have already identified their next leaders and are working very deliberately to develop them. This practice is especially important for family-owned firms.

Developing leaders from within the firm appears to be one of the key differentiating factors in sustaining a business for the long term. The old companies are concerned not just about reaping today's harvest, they are cultivating the ground for future crops. This factor is especially apparent in the area of leadership development. As Arie de Geus describes in *The Living Company*, "No matter how widely diversified they were, their [the old companies] employees (and even their suppliers, at times) felt they were all part of one entity. This cohesion around the idea of 'community' meant that managers were typically chosen for advancement from within; they succeeded through the generational flow of members and considered themselves stewards of the longstanding enterprise."

Ben Salzmann, CEO and President of 90-year old insurance company Acuity, No. 3 on the 2015 list of *Fortune*'s "Best Companies to Work For" (and a company with full-time turnover of just one percent), sums up the employee relations longevity factor well. "It's not about 'employees.' It's about you, you personally. I want to engage you. I want to have you set new aspirations and surpass them. I want you to be delighted in what you do."

Active Members of the Local Community

5

Hoekstra's Hardware (1867)

There's still a future for the independent, local hardware store. And to me, that future is a good one. We do a lot of business with both the businesses nearby and the people who live in the surrounding neighborhoods. People always ask us, 'Why don't you move?' We feel like this is where we've been and this is the place to be. This is home. (Phil Ippel, Encore West Michigan Magazine *interview*)

The Mutual Assurance Society of Virginia (1794)

The Mutual Assurance Society of Virginia has a long history of benevolent support for the communities in which it does business. From its early history of donating fire-fighting equipment to the City of Richmond and contributions to cities throughout Virginia in support of the development of central water systems for fire suppression, to the Society's support of United Way organizations in every city in which it does business, we have demonstrated an unfailing commitment to the good of society.

Carrollton Bank (1877)

[One of the values that shape our actions is] "Be a friend and neighbor: After my Great Uncle John died in 1960, we found something amazing. A drawer with a big stack of personal notes in it—loans ranging from $100 to $1,000 that added up to almost $50,000. The Depression made it almost impossible for banks to give families the loans they needed. But when a Carrollton family desperately needed financial help, Uncle John would quietly take them into his office and make them a loan out of his own pocket. He never told anyone about this. He just helped his neighbors. (Tom Hough, CEO)

Because Century Club companies see themselves as integral parts of webs of relationships often connected to their family history and reputation, the development of relationships within the local community—both commercial and social—is just as important as the development of relationships with their business partners. The old companies actively participate in their local communities, promoting them and developing local networks for mutual learning and benefit. In many cases a company and its local community are so closely associated with each other that they are seen as one and the same. Duarte's Tavern in Pescadero, California is a fourth generation family business that exemplifies the deep connection to community often found in old companies.

Frank Duarte established the business as a saloon and barbershop in 1894. The tavern soon offered food for locals and weekenders too. Frank's grandson Ron Duarte and his wife Lynn first experimented with their famous Cream of Artichoke soup in the early 1960s. Today, Duarte's is a family and community business, run by the fourth generation of the Duarte family. We were a local destination in Pescadero's heyday in the 1920s, [today] we still brew the day's first cup of coffee for local farmers. Generations of families have grown up working with us in the restaurant, tavern or garden. Most of our full-time staff have been with us many years and live within walking distance of the tavern. Pescadero is a coastal farming community and Duarte's is where friends meet.

Sometimes the company or a product brand name becomes intertwined with the community in which they operate. Such is the case with Ye Olde Pepper Company (1806), a 200-year-old company run by the fourth generation of the family that bought the company around the turn of the 20th century. Its Gibralter mints, which the company claims to be the oldest commercially made candy in the United States, are closely identified with the city of Salem, Massachusetts as described on their website.

Historic Salem, Massachusetts immediately suggests Hawthorne, witchcraft and a once-prosperous seaport. Besides these interesting features there is a delight in associating the toothsome Gibralter with this old city. Crossing the North Bridge we are reminded by the sense of smell that we are in the vicinity of one of Salem's most noted productions, Salem Gibralters. When one is enjoying the purity and delicious flavor of this confection, it is hard to realize that they are made and wrapped in exactly the same way as sold by Mrs. Spencer from a pail, on the steps of the Old First Church, over 200 years ago.

Century Club companies score significantly higher than young firms on every research question relating to building relationships within their communities. Whether it was participating in business organizations such as the Chamber of Commerce, building personal connections with people in other industries, or being involved in projects to promote their local community, the older firms are significant, active members of their communities. They see the positive effects that result from connections with local people in other industries. They also believe their business positively influences the local community's reputation—and that the local community's good reputation helps their business. One might expect such community commitment from a local bank, and the focus on building their community for the long term has kept organizations such as Bath Savings Institution thriving since 1852. (Notice the way they also tie in their commitment to employees as part of the web of relationships that has led to their success.)

Beyond a financial institution, we're neighbors who care. We invest in what matters most—the people, places and businesses that make Maine the place we're proud to call home. When you entrust us with your savings, we keep your money here in Maine, where it belongs. We use your deposits to help neighbors buy homes, entrepreneurs start businesses, and non-profits make a difference. We believe in building relationships that last for generations by providing exceptional service and sound solutions customized to meet the individual needs of our customers. Bath Savings is proud to be recognized as one of the Best Places to Work in Maine and we believe it is our employees who make Bath Savings such a great place to work and bank.

As a result of recognizing the value provided by the society beyond their individual business or industry, the old companies invest time and resources in projects that develop and sustain their communities. And when a crisis hits, the old companies are there to help. In 2010 when a break in an oil pipeline (the largest and costliest inland oil spill in U.S. history) created a crisis in the town of Marshall, Michigan, fourth generation Schuler's Restaurant (1909) responded by ramping up to feed over 2500 meals to clean-up crews, and they did this around the clock, each day, at multiple locations throughout their community—for months.

Such community support works both ways. Here's the story of 150-year-old, sixth-generation Breitbach's Country Dining (1852) in Balltown, Iowa, which was struck by fire and completely destroyed twice within 18 months. In this case, the community helped rescue the business.

The first fire happened on December 24th, 2007. The family and this small community and many others who had visited the family restaurant were devastated. It didn't take long for this community to rally around the Breitbach family in the process of rebuilding the restaurant that had become an icon of their community, and less than six months after the fire a new restaurant was up and running. Bus-loads of people came from all over Iowa, Wisconsin, Minnesota, Illinois and other parts of the country to see the work the community had helped build and enjoy the same home-style cooking they had previously known. Then, ten months to the day after the first fire, Mike Breitbach once again received a call that his building was on fire. The business that had been built by love and community was now gone, again. After the second fire, the thought of rebuilding was more difficult. The

> *family and the whole community were in shock. Everyone*
> *waited, and just before Christmas 2008 Mike and his family*
> *announced they would once again rebuild Iowa's oldest*
> *bar and restaurant, and the community once again rallied*
> *around the Breitbach family. On August 1, 2009 people from*
> *everywhere flooded the small town of Balltown as Breitbach's*
> *Country Dining reopened its doors. (You can see more of this*
> *remarkable story in the film* Spinning Plates.*)*

Often when I talk about social responsibility with my
students, they think in terms of philanthropy or monetary
donations to non-profit organizations, and they ask how
small or start-up companies can do this when they are still
struggling to be profitable themselves. The community
relationship practices engaged in by Century Club
companies are great examples of how social responsibility
and community service can be more than financial donations
to the United Way, although when able, the old companies
are philanthropic as well. Often these practices take the
form of supporting employees' volunteer efforts, such as this
example from King Arthur Flour Company (1790).

> *Our volunteer program encourages employee-owners to*
> *spend time helping nonprofit organizations here in Vermont*
> *and beyond by providing paid time off for volunteering*
> *during normal work hours. Paid volunteer time may seem an*
> *oxymoron, but we've found that allowing folks to dedicate*
> *some of their working hours to causes they support gives*
> *busy people a chance to do something they may not*
> *otherwise have time for, and often inspires folks to dedicate*
> *even more time to helping their communities. We provide 40*
> *hours of paid volunteer time per year to part-time and full-*
> *time employees.*

Other companies have "donated" their employees to non-
profits during slow times in the business cycle, thus keeping
valued people on their payroll when business turns up
again while also contributing to their community. It would
be difficult to overstate the loyalty and dedication that
these practices create in employees, who become *bona*

fide and admired community members, as well as long-term contributors to their companies.

John Bachman, current owner of eighth-generation, family-run Bachman Funeral Home (1769) says he is driven by the same thing that motivated the founder hundreds of years ago—community. "There's a certain amount of pride in this job," said Bachman. "It's about feeling respected, appreciated and about helping people around you." The fifth generation leader of Harden Furniture (1844) describes his company's relationship with its local community over the years.

> *As the family legacy endures, Harden Furniture continues to grow and change in order to best serve those customers who desire fine furniture from generation to generation... at just the right value. The story of Harden is much more than the history of a furniture company and a family. . . it reflects the history of our region and our country, and it has directly shaped the history of a community. From the very beginning, Frank's concern for his employees and the village in which they lived was reflected in the construction of churches, a community house, and several homes for the employees. This tradition has continued over the years, with the building of a fire department, a golf course, and a new post office.*

Many of the Century Club companies are small- to medium-size businesses with a single location, and the local community is intertwined with the history of their company—and often the story of the family that started or owns the company. But what about businesses that have expanded into multiple locations? What does this longevity factor look like in these companies? An interesting example is Glik's (1897), a clothing retailer in more than 60 locations across Midwest America. The company began with the idea of selling top-quality merchandise in rural areas of Missouri and Iowa, and their motto today is still "Big City Fashion. Small Town Service." They credit their success to bringing fashion-forward, name brand apparel and strong customer service to Midwest hometown markets. Members of the Glik family personally select each location for a new store. But they don't stock a new store with standard inventory. They specifically select merchandise for each locale; no two Glik's stores are ever the same. Then store managers are given the decision-making authority that encourages them to develop close ties with their communities and focus 100 percent on the personal customer service that the Gliks say built their company.

Unexpectedly, we discovered this longevity factor of community often extends beyond the immediate neighborhood, city, or state where a company is located. Many of the century-old companies are also at the forefront of environmental practices. Who knew that being an environmental sustainability leader would be a distinguishing factor of old companies? We didn't expect it. We didn't even ask about environment efforts in our initial research. We should perhaps have had a clue, based on the commitment of Century Club companies to their communities, as well as the fact that they have an attitude of stewardship regarding sustaining their business. But the fact is, I came across this factor by accident.

One of the courses I teach is called Managing for Environmental Sustainability. In prepping for the course I ordered a book I thought would be good for our business students called *Green to Gold: How Smart Companies Use Environmental Strategy to Innovate, Create Value, and Build Competitive Advantage* by Daniel Esty and Andrew Winston. The authors list companies they consider forward-thinking in the area of sustainable business practices, calling them "wave makers." As I was reading through the list, I recognized a number of the names from my database of 100-year-old companies! Most people assume that a "green" strategy is something new and entrepreneurial, but it turns out Century Club businesses commonly include sustainability in their values and practices.

The more I thought about this, the more sense it made. The stewardship attitude of leaders in the old companies frames their role as preserving the firm for future generations. It's a logical extension of this leadership philosophy to include preserving the environment for future generations. Old companies' environmental sustainability strategies likely arise from their sense of social responsibility to their communities. As Sawyer Bentwood (1801) says:

> *Our factory is located in the quiet town of Whitingham in rural Vermont, where nature abounds; our rural location is a testimony to our love and respect for the outdoors. Sawyer Bentwood is committed to reducing wood and water waste; we work in partnership with local businesses to help reduce our collective ecological footprint.*

For some Century Club companies, environmental practices are the very core of their business, such as Louis Padnos Iron & Metal Company (1905) whose business is recycling. E. Butterworth & Co. (1839) has been a recycler of textiles for its entire history and is one of the oldest companies in the world handling textile by-products and recycled textile waste.

The environmental practices of Century Club companies may also stem from their frugality. Though sustainable business practices often require up-front investments, they usually save money in the long run. Since these companies intend to be around for the long term, they know they will benefit from the investment.

Once sustaining the company becomes part of the DNA of a firm, long-term, perhaps holistic thinking becomes an overriding factor in every decision. As Levi Strauss & Co. (1853) says, "Using innovative, sustainable, and progressive practices isn't just how we make our jeans and other products, it's a principle we value in all of our work."

Once I began looking for it, I saw this leading-edge attitude toward environmental sustainability in almost every Century Club company I studied. When I visited cruise ship manufacturer Meyer Werft (1795) in the summer of 2014, its head of R&D mentioned that the company was developing fuel cell technology to power ships. He said they didn't expect it to be viable for 20 years or so, but they were investing in the project because they felt it was the best way to address the issue of how to power big ships in an environmentally responsible manner. With a 20-year timeframe and based on a belief in finding the best solution to an environmental issue, who other than a very profitable 200-year-old company would make such an investment? This is an example of the innovative strategies of old companies. They innovate and change, or they wouldn't have survived for so long. Their belief in stewardship makes innovation, including in environmentally sustainable practices, a way to ensure their viability into the future. The attitude of stewardship among Century Club companies also dovetails with their belief in holistic and connected businesses partners and communities. Century Club members see themselves as only one part of a web of interconnected interests. What benefits one part, should benefit all.

More confirmation of the longevity and environmental sustainability connection came with the 2015 list of the "Global 100 Most Sustainable Corporations in the World," an index prepared by the Corporate Knights organization. Though fewer than one percent of all U.S. companies are over 100 years old, 40 percent of the U.S. firms on the Corporate Knights' list are over 100! If one defines "longevity" as companies over 90 years old, 50 percent of the U.S. companies on this list are long-term sustainability leaders.

As I've said before, many of the Century Club companies are not large businesses. But this hasn't stopped them from being at the forefront of environmental sustainability. Here is what paper manufacturer Crane & Co. (1855), manufacturer of fine stationery, national currency, and security papers for over 200 years, has to say.

> *All manufacturing processes operate with environmental consequences. The challenge is to minimize our footprint on the environment and continuously search for ways to improve. Long before it became fashionable or required by law, we took aggressive and expensive measures to reduce our impact on the environment. Over the years, our pollution-prevention efforts have been recognized by environmental organizations and the Commonwealth of Massachusetts as being at the forefront of the industry. Despite our relatively small size, we have full-time staff devoted to waste minimization, chemical reduction and substitution, water and energy reduction, and renewable energy research. 70 percent of the energy used to make paper in Dalton comes from municipal waste. The waste fibers from our papermaking processes are not sent to landfills, nor are they burned. We compost them with municipal leaf and yard waste to create topsoil for land reclamation projects.*

The deep relationships old companies have with their local communities, as well as their long-term view of business, seem to naturally lead to a concern for the sustainability of the environment around them that nurtures and supports their business—whether that environment is human, manmade, or natural. As the leadership of King Arthur Flour says,

> *We strive every day to be good stewards, identifying and implementing ways to improve our environmental footprint, providing funding and service to community organizations, nurturing an employee-focused ownership culture, and maintaining the highest standards for our products and services.*

Or, as the paper manufacturer Crane & Co. explains,

> *Crane is a family-owned company, doing business in the same location for over 200 years—a community in which generations of our families continue to live and work. It's our home. We do our best to keep it neat and clean.*

Seeing themselves as part of an interconnected ecosystem—something larger than their own business—is a defining Century Club characteristic. This combination of humility and obligation leads to long-term thinking and decisions that take into account far-reaching effects. Strong community connections and environment advocacy are then natural emphases for Century Club members. To paraphrase John Donne, no company is an island. Century Club members see that truth, act on it, and in part survive because of it. If I were to single out one unique longevity characteristic that resulted from our research, this is it.

COMMON
QUESTIONS

Over the years of presenting this research to both academic and business audiences, I have noticed some recurring questions. Assuming you may be wondering about similar issues, I will try to address them. If you have other questions, please contact me at CenturyClubCompanies@gmail.com. I expect my research into these admirable companies will continue, and I'd welcome you to join me digitally.

What about Schumpeter's theory of creative destruction? Don't some companies need to 'die' to make way for progress?

Free market economists tend to dismiss the value of longevity. They maintain the old need to die to make way for the new, that vanishing companies and lost jobs are inherent parts of a growing economic system. Yes, there is a natural process of corporate death, but too many companies die prematurely, and it is these premature deaths which devastate people's lives, communities, and economies. Companies should survive to contribute to society the productivity of their mature years. (See the arguments from deGeus and Hamel described in the Introduction). No one could speak to this issue more eloquently than former McKinsey managing director Ian Davis in his reflections on corporate longevity published in the September 2014 issue of *McKinsey Quarterly*.

> *Not all destruction is creative, and not all creativity is destructive. The demise of a company is not damaging only for its stakeholders. Sometimes, it may also be an inefficient way of innovating in the economy or an industry, because it breaks up established and tangible assets, such as R&D know-how and strong consumer and supplier relationships. A company that learns to adapt and change to meet market demands avoids not just the trauma of decline or an unwanted change of ownership but also very real transaction and disruption costs.*

Is there a natural life span for a business?

It has been estimated that the natural average life span of a corporation could be as long as 200-300 years. There are several companies in Europe and Asia this age and older. Yet the current average age of companies in the United States is 12-15 years. Perhaps longevity is simply not a goal for the leaders of many American companies. Or, perhaps companies die prematurely because managers don't know what factors increase longevity and therefore have not put in place the practices that would increase their company's chances of survival. Since managers do not seek or cultivate the habits needed for long-term survival, many companies do not live as long as they could, to the detriment of many of their stakeholders. By identifying, monitoring, and implementing the right practices, we humans have increased our life span over 80 percent in just one century. In addition to medical advances, we have learned what behaviors increase longevity: a balanced diet, regular exercise, monitoring key measures such as blood pressure, cholesterol, and so on. In spite of the complexities of corporate life, research has identified some very specific practices that could result in longer-lived corporations.

When a company dies a "natural" death it looks more like the following story of a furniture company that closed after over 130 years in business. Facing increasing cost pressures from offshore manufacturers, and with no one in the next generation interested in running the business, this family-owned furniture manufacturer decided it needed to close.

After spending quite a bit of time explaining to employees the decision, a public announcement was made. Three TV stations and two newspapers immediately showed up at the company site. The company owner and president told the media he couldn't deal with all of them, so he gave the news teams the run of the place. They took full advantage of the opportunity, interviewing and filming dozens of employees. The TV reporter said he's covered over 100 plant closings and this was the only one where not one person had a bad thing to say about the company. He concluded his evening news report with this: "They say your name doesn't have to be on the door to be part of this family company. You get the feeling it really is that way." Following the announcement that the factory would be closing, productivity actually went up and quality reached levels of near perfection. When employees were asked about this, they related a determination to make products they could always be proud of and to finish well. Area companies worked closely with the firm to identify job openings that matched the skills and ambitions of the employees and most people affected by the closing landed on their feet.

When people and communities live through the death of a business, it can be traumatic or it can be a natural passage. When old companies face difficult change, including the time to say good-bye, they realize the need to help each other through such transitions—and to celebrate a long "life" well-lived.

What role does leadership play in corporate longevity?

One of the questions I receive most frequently about the characteristics and behaviors of companies that have survived over 100 years concerns particular leadership behaviors among Century Club companies. The short answer is that no consistent leadership qualities emerged from the research. Most companies revere their founders or other leaders who led the company during a critical juncture in the firm's history. And most of these companies have leaders who have grown up in the company, which usually produces some consistency in leadership style within a particular organization. But there was not any consistency in leadership behaviors across the organizations we surveyed. What did seem important was that leaders follow the principles of longevity, including embodying the corporate culture and its values in themselves.

Like all companies, Century Club firms face crises. Almost every one we talked to related a story about the time the company overcame great obstacles to continue to live another day. These stories often describe heroics on the part of the founder or key salesperson or some other leader. But they also describe how employees or suppliers sacrificed to help the organization survive rough times, or how customers or the local community provided support to recover from a disaster.

Of course leadership matters, and these old companies, as with other firms, thrive under astute leaders who make good business decisions. But the Century Club companies also seem to survive under weak leadership, as long as the core principles of the longevity model are not violated. Increasingly, companies are beginning to realize that this collective force of a company's culture can be more powerful than individual leaders. Deloitte's annual survey of 3,300 executives in 106 countries found that top managers said preserving and strengthening culture is the most important issue they face, even more important than leadership.

Does keeping a company in the family, or at least privately owned, make a difference in longevity?

Every privately-owned Century Club company interviewed said staying private was key to their longevity. They felt being private enabled them to chart their own course, rather than having to "dance to Wall Street's tune." *The Economist* calculates that the majority of the world's most successful medium-size companies are family firms and account for two-thirds of Germany's Mittelstand. Family owners typically want their firms to last for generations, and they can make long-term investments without worrying about shareholders looking for short-term profits. However, when analyzing our U.S. database of 100-year-old companies, we found that the percentage of privately-owned firms was no greater than their representation in the general business population. There are more than a few successful public firms over 100 years old. In several of them members of the founding family still wield significant clout. Even if the family doesn't hold a majority of shares, family members often are board members and influence the choice of chief executive. A 2014 *The Economist* article describes the positive influence family ownership or involvement can have on a business:

> *Whether private or public, family firms tend to take a longer-term perspective. . . . Non-family-controlled public companies tend to be obsessed with meeting the demands of investors to maximise short-term profits. . . . There is evidence of a positive 'family effect' on financial performance equivalent to five percentage points of extra return per year. The presence of a founding family seems to be good for a business's image. In a recent survey by Heinz-Peter Elstrodt of McKinsey, 73 percent of people said they trusted family-owned companies, compared with 64 percent who trusted publicly-traded companies.*

Though publicly-traded companies can—and do—survive for the long run, there does seem to be a benefit to remaining privately owned if longevity is a desired goal. The advantage of privately-owned firms is their sense of ownership. This helps them get around a major aspect of many businesses that interferes with longevity, the focus on short-term results and the potential conflict of interest between shareholders and managers.

Isn't the purpose of every company to maximize profits? Why do you downplay the role of profits in the longevity model?

One of the longevity practices of old companies that produces skepticism among managers and academics, particularly those with a financial background, is how seldom making money is stated as the chief purpose of the business. Old companies often talk about the purpose or goal of their business in lofty terms that seem soft and idealistic to operational managers. The old companies are certainly concerned about profitability. They readily concede the necessity of profits, but they look at them as the fuel to keep their company "engine" operating rather than their destination. Century Club companies are profitable; they wouldn't have survived for over 100 years if they weren't. If they have to choose between profits and growth, they will choose profits. However, maximizing profits is not seen as the primary purpose of their business. As one CEO put it, "I need to eat to survive, but that doesn't mean my focus in life should be maximizing my consumption of food. Eating enough to stay healthy is sufficient."

Here is a nice comment on this question from Mark Gunther's book *Faith and Fortune*.

> As architects of great companies, James C. Penney [company founded 1902] and Milton S. Hershey [company founded 1894] were in some respects ahead of their time. Each man imbued his company with a purpose that was more inspiring than making money. Both knew that profits were essential, but profits were not the reason to do business. They saw their role as serving their workers and their customers, as well as making money for themselves and their owners. . . . They managed not for the next quarter, but for the next quarter of a century.

In Japan, where my research partner was able to obtain profitability data even from small privately-owned firms, companies over 100 years old were twice as profitable as the average Japanese firm. In Christopher Stadler's research, old European companies were also more profitable than their younger counterparts. I have not been able to obtain such data from U.S. companies, but I have no reason to believe they are any different.

The point is not that that the old companies don't see profits as important, but that they view them from a different perspective. Accomplishing their mission and purpose comes first. If the company does this well, making money will follow. As Harish Manwani, COO of Unilever (1885) discusses in a YouTube video, "Profit isn't enough to sustain a business. You need businesses that can actually define their role in society in terms of a much larger purpose than the products and brands that they sell. Values and purpose are going to be the two drivers that create the companies of tomorrow."

CONCLUSION

Graybar (1869)

From its humble beginnings as a small shop in Cleveland to the multi-billion-dollar organization Graybar has become, its philosophy of working to the advantage of its customers, suppliers, employees, shareholders and communities continues to withstand the test of time.

It is no coincidence that three of the five factors in the longevity model have to do with relationships. The emphasis on relationships among Century Club companies shapes their cultures. Most Century Club companies' mission statements or credos describe the relationships they desire with customers, employees, and business partners. They extend the idea of "relationship" to include the communities they see as part of their world and even to the natural environment. Though some businesspeople may view building relationships as a "soft" practice, it clearly differentiates 100-year-old companies from shorter-lived organizations. Editorials in every issue of *Fortune*'s "100 Best Companies to Work For" emphasize this connection between relationships and workplace culture to business success. Relationships are at the core of how old companies operate. They regard the maintenance of relationships with employees, customers, suppliers, and others in their community from generation to generation as the foundation for their long-term success. They see themselves as one part of a larger system or interconnected web, and they truly believe they cannot maintain their success for long periods of time without the cooperation of others. Here is what the current president and CEO of a 160-year-old community bank says.

Through the years, Essex Savings Bank has played a vital part in the lives of those in the communities we serve. We've taken pride in helping our customers build their homes, educate their children and create livelihoods that contribute to the prosperity of the Connecticut River Valley. . . . Through the years, we've never lost sight of our forefathers' goal—a commitment to personal relationships. More than a century and a half has passed and we have never wavered from that promise. We continue our long heritage as a mutual savings bank, a non-public organization with a far-reaching vision for our customers and the communities we serve. Our Community Investment Program, which returns 10 percent of our net income to non-profits, is a testament to our commitment.

> *We wish to thank our customers, directors, trustees, officers and employees who support our mission to continue to provide service and trust to our community.*

Or this, from Northwestern Mutual (1857).

> *Relationships are built on trust. Our lives and businesses matter. And we're much stronger together than apart. We create meaningful employment opportunities and invest in our people. We strengthen local businesses and economies. We give back. Help out. These beliefs are hardwired into our DNA: Doing what's right. Taking the long-term view. Sharing our success.*

Many of the significant behaviors exhibited by old companies preceded the recent development of stakeholder theory, defined as "obtaining a competitive advantage through the development of close-knit ties with a broad range of internal and external constituencies," rather than focusing primarily on meeting the desires of shareholders. In particular, Century Club companies practice a mutual learning form of stakeholder theory, one in which a company acknowledges the interdependency of the firm and its stakeholders and uses the relationships to understand each group's needs, combine resources, and find solutions to create value for all parties involved. As early as 1947, Forrest E. Mars, Sr. stated his objective to build a business that manufactured and distributed food products in a manner that created a "mutuality of benefits" for all stakeholders. Mars (1911) is still owned by the Mars family and remains committed to this objective. They say they "plan for the long term" and make choices now that will help them "grow sustainably for generations to come."

This idea of shared value has recently been described by Michael Porter and Mark Kramer as the next evolution of capitalism. "Companies must take the lead in bringing business and society back together. . . . The solution lies in the principle of shared value, which involves creating economic value in a way that also creates value for society by addressing its needs and challenges." They say companies that optimize short-term financial performance while ignoring the factors of long-term success are trapped in an outdated approach to value creation. "Shared value is. . . a new way to achieve economic success." [*Harvard Business Review* January–February 2011]

Companies that have thrived for over 100 years have been successfully practicing such a form of capitalism that creates shared value for a very long time. Shared value is perhaps not so much a new theory to achieve economic success as a rediscovered approach that Century Club companies have quietly been using for over a century.

Some old companies have chosen to formalize and publicly affirm this idea of shared value or stakeholder theory by becoming a Benefit Corporation. The Benefit Corporation, or "B Corp," is a type of for-profit corporate entity legislated in 27 states in the U.S. The purpose of a B Corp includes creating general public benefit, so companies include as their legally defined goals a positive impact on society and the environment in addition to profit. In 2007, 100 percent employee-owned 225-year old King Arthur Flour Co. changed its bylaws to become a B Corp, saying this reflects its commitment to all stakeholders including shareholders, business partners, the community, and the environment.

Leaders of the century-old companies believe all five of the factors described in our longevity model must be implemented together to achieve a successful business over the long term. This reflects the holistic approach the leaders in the Century Club companies take to running their businesses. Don't focus too much on customers and ignore your employees (or vice versa). Don't invest in developing your company's core competencies without also helping your community thrive (or vice versa). Don't change so fast that you forget to honor the traditions that got you to this point (or be so stuck in tradition that you don't change). Only the practice of all five factors and a deft balancing of them leads to long-term success. The web of interaction formed by these factors creates the culture of a company—the way people within the firm behave without being told. King Arthur Flour Company (1790) says this quite well when they describe why they became a Beneficial Corporation.

> *We're committed to treating our customers and partners, our community, and the natural environment with as much care as we give to maintaining the high quality of our flour. After all, healthy relationships with all of these stakeholders will enable our centuries-old business to continue working toward our mission for another 200 years.*

This emphasis on relationships with all stakeholders leads to a kind of symbiosis with organizations outside the company and significantly improves the company's ability to weather challenges as well as learn and adapt over time. As Judith Rosener says in her 1990 Harvard Business Review article "Ways Women Lead": ". . . business runs better when people within an organization know and trust one another—deals move faster and more smoothly, teams are more productive, people learn more quickly and perform with more creativity. . . . Strong relationships, most managers will agree, are the grease of an organization."

Cranston Print Works (1807) sums up the connections among all the longevity factors quite well.

> *Cranston is an employee-owned company whose fundamental and on-going mission is to continue to serve the needs of its customers, employees and the society in which we live. We look forward to continuing our commitment to the environment, our local communities and to our customers. After all, 'quality' is not just a byword at Cranston Print Works—it's a centuries-old tradition!*

In the end, sustaining a business for the long term may simply come down to intent. The leaders and followers of these old companies have decided they want their firm to "live" a long life and this goal drives them to make decisions and take actions that are quite different from those in organizations whose main objective is to maximize profits or grow to a certain size. Collins and Porras mention this factor in their book *Built to Last*, which they referred to as a focus on building the company. "The company itself is seen as the ultimate creation, not specific ideas, products or personal wealth." The authors said they had to shift their thinking from seeing a company as a vehicle for products to seeing products as a vehicle for a company.

Here is such a statement of intent from a 160-year-old milling company. "We are committed to the stewardship and growth of C.H. Guenther & Son, Inc., and the preservation of its heritage, independence, and family ownership." Or, as Hussey Seating Company (1835) states on its website:

> *There have been six generations of continuous Hussey family leadership, and the seventh generation is beginning to show up for summer employment and hopefully more. One of the major benefits of a family business is the long-term perspective towards the future. The family owners view themselves as stewards of the legacy, and can make important decisions for the long run. We are a family business in it for the long run.*

Survival over the long term may be the ultimate measure of organizational and leadership performance. Long-term survival tests the value, relevance, resiliency, and creativity of an organization in ways that short-term financial performance does not. *The Fifth Discipline* author and systems thinking expert, Peter Senge, talks about the problem of "dynamic complexity" in organizations today. He says the effect of most management decisions are far removed in time (and space) from when (and often who and where) a decision is made. So what looks like a good result from a decision in the short term may end up being disastrous for the firm (and those connected to it) in the long run. Our study of Century Club companies has convinced me that survival over the long term is the true measure of a company's success. Only if the company's practices, products, and services make a real and lasting contribution to society will it survive.

Once sustaining a business becomes the major criterion for success, who wants to be the leader during the company's demise? Such leaders fail not only the company and its employees, they devastate the web of customers, business partners, and communities so intricately connected to Century Club companies. The integrated implementation of these practices has proven to invigorate and sustain organizations over decades, not three-month quarters.

If you viewed your company leadership or contributor role as one of stewardship, how might your behavior and practices change? If your legacy depended on successfully shepherding the business and handing it over in great shape to the next generation, would you make different decisions today? One thing we learned from the Century Club companies: the first step is deciding that survival is the ultimate goal. From there, the five practices forming the longevity model can help you reach it.

THE
CENTURY CLUB
COMPANIES

Here is a list of U.S. companies over 100 years old identified as of 2015. Because so many Century Club companies are small and privately owned, it is difficult to discover all those that should be on this list. It is my desire to frequently update this book, so I would appreciate any information on companies that should be added to this list. If you know of a for-profit business that has been in continuous operation as an independent company for over 100 years, please contact me at CenturyClubCompanies@gmail.com. I also love hearing stories about Century Club companies!

As noted earlier, just because these companies are old does not mean they will live forever. It is entirely possible that by the time this book goes into print, some of the firms listed will have died a natural death or been acquired/ merged into a different entity. I would appreciate hearing that information as well.

● Zildjian	Norwell	MA	1623
● The John Stevens Shop	Newport	RI	1705
● Lakeside Mills	Spindale	NC	1736
● Caswell-Massey	Edison	NJ	1752
● Philadelphia Contributionship	Philadelphia	PA	1752
● Seaside Inn	Kennebunkport	ME	1756
● Beekman Arms	Rhinebeck	NY	1766
● Bachman Funeral Home	Strasburg	PA	1769
● Tower Publishing	Standish	ME	1772
● Laird & Company	Scobeyville	NJ	1780
● D. Landreth Seed Company	New Freedom	PA	1784
● Bixler's Jewelers	Allentown	PA	1785
● Hayes Coffee	Oak Park	IL	1787
● George R. Ruhl & Son	Hanover	MD	1789
● King Arthur Flour Company	Norwich	VT	1790
● Cadwalader, Wickersham & Taft	New York	NY	1792
● Baltimore Equitable Insurance	Baltimore	MD	1794
● Mutual Assurance Society of Virginia	Richmond	VA	1794
● Birkett Mills	Penn Yan	NY	1797
● Gruber Almanac	Mercersburg	PA	1797
● Wayside Inn	Middletown	VA	1797
● Alan McIlvain Company	Marcus Hook	PA	1798
● Crane & Co.	Dalton	MA	1801
● Sawyer Bentwood	Whitingham	VT	1801
★ DuPont	Wilmington	DE	1802
● Emmet, Marvin & Martin	New York	NY	1805
★ Valspar	Minneapolis	MN	1806
● Ye Olde Pepper Candy Companie	Salem	MA	1806
● Cranston Print Works	Cranston	RI	1807
★ John Wiley & Sons	Hoboken	NJ	1807
● Rider's Inn	Painesville	OH	1812

The Century Club Companies

• Cooper, Erving & Savage	Albany	NY	1813
• Loane Brothers	Towson	MD	1815
• Hodgdon Yachts	East Boothbay	ME	1816
∗ York Water Co	York	PA	1816
• Claflin	Warwick	RI	1817
• Brown Brothers Harriman	New York	NY	1818
• Eaton Funeral Homes	Newton	MA	1818
∗ Libbey Inc.	Toledo	OH	1818
• The Bromwell Company	Los Angeles	CA	1819
• Comstock, Ferre & Company	Wethersfield	CT	1820
• Rose Law Firm	Little Rock	AR	1820
• Bartlett Yarns	Harmony	ME	1821
• Hickok & Boardman Insurance	Burlington	VT	1821
• Inquirer and Mirror	Nantucket	MA	1821
• Mayfair Bakery	Philadelphia	PA	1823
• Munson Machinery Company	Utica	NY	1823
• New Hope Mills	Auburn	NY	1823
• Ashaway Line & Twine Mfg. Co.	Ashaway	RI	1824
• John Baer's Sons	Lancaster	PA	1825
• M.A. Patout & Son	Jeanerette	LA	1825
• C.S. Osborne	Harrison	NJ	1826
• Cincinnati Equitable Companies	Cincinnati	OH	1826
• Union Oyster House	Boston	MA	1826
• Middlebury Inn	Middlebury	VT	1827
• Saco and Biddeford Savings	Saco	ME	1827
• William H. Jackson Company	New York	NY	1827
• Centreville Bank	West Warick	RI	1828
• Cornell Iron Works	Mountaintop	PA	1828
• George Jerome & Co.	Roseville	MI	1828
• Vermont Mutual Insurance	Montpelier	VT	1828
• Yuengling Brewery	Pottsville	PA	1829

● Curtis Mallet-Prevost, Colt & Mosle	New York	NY	1830
● E.A. Clore Sons	Madison	VA	1830
● Woolrich	Woolrich	PA	1830
● Bevin Bros. Manufacturing Co.	East Hampton	CT	1832
★ Rogers Corporation	Rogers	CT	1832
● Saucon Mutual Insurance	Bethlehem	PA	1832
● Simonds International	Fitchburg	MA	1832
● C. F. Martin & Co.	Nazareth	PA	1833
● Century House	Nantucket	MA	1833
● Green Mountain Inn	Stowe	VT	1833
● Champion Sailmakers	Freeport	NY	1834
★ Hingham Institution for Savings	Hingham	MA	1834
● Hinkle Chair Company	Greenbrier	TN	1834
● McGuireWoods	Richmond	VA	1834
● Hussey Seating Co.	North Berwick	ME	1835
● McLanahan	Holidaysburg	PA	1835
● Toledo Blade	Toledo	OH	1835
● Bromberg's	Birmingham	AL	1836
● Stevenson Manufacturing	Wellsville	OH	1836
● The Calais Advertiser	Calais	ME	1836
● Belcher Corporation	South Easton	MA	1837
● Deere & Company	Moline	IL	1837
● Delmonico's	New York	NY	1837
● Higgins, Roberts & Suprunowicz	Schenectady	NY	1837
● Morse Diving	Rockland	MA	1837
★ Procter & Gamble	Cincinnati	OH	1837
★ Tiffany & Co.	New York	NY	1837
★ Ballston Spa Bancorp	Ballston Spa	NY	1838
● C.O. Bigelow	New York	NY	1838
● Comstock Castle Stove Co.	Quincy	IL	1838
● Merrow Sewing Machine Co.	Fall River	MA	1838

• E.B. Horn	Boston	MA	1839
• Moulton Ladder & Supply Company	Philadelphia	PA	1839
• Schaeffer Manufacturing	St. Louis	MO	1839
• Suter's Handcrafted Furniture	Harrisonburg	VA	1839
• Antoine's Restaurant	New Orleans	LA	1840
• Gillies Coffee Company	New York	NY	1840
• Stephen Hillenmeyer Landscape Services	Lexington	KY	1841
• Glades Pike Inn	Somerset	PA	1842
• Hildreth's Home Goods	Southhampton	NY	1842
• Johnson Woolen Mill	Johnson	VT	1842
• Rugg Manufacturing Co.	Leominster	MA	1842
★ SI Financial Group	Willimantic	CT	1842
• Verdin Company	Cincinnati	OH	1842
• Frederick Mutual Insurance	Frederick	MD	1843
• John Baumann Safe Co.	St. Louis	MO	1843
• Shelby County Newspapers	Columbiana	AL	1843
• Harden Furniture	McConnellsville	NY	1844
★ Brunswick Corporation	Lake Forest	IL	1845
• New York Life Insurance Company	New York	NY	1845
★ Church & Dwight Co.	Ewing	NJ	1846
• Gulick's Illiana Medical Equip & Supply	Danville	IL	1846
• Martin's Shoe House	Monroe	MI	1846
• Powell Valves	Cincinnati	OH	1846
• Yaeger's Shoes	Monroe	MI	1846
• Zophar Mills	Amityville	NY	1846
• Annin Flagmakers	Roseland	NJ	1847
• Brierly Lombard and Company	Worcester	MA	1847
• C.W. Estes Company	Fairfield	NJ	1847
• Faller's Furniture	Clarion	PA	1847
• Freeman Funeral Homes	Manalapan	NJ	1847
• McCarter & English	Newark	NJ	1847

● Stinson's Jewelers	Camden	AR	1847
● Hancock Lumber Company	Casco	ME	1848
● Macomber, Farr & Whitten	Augusta	ME	1848
● Maze Lumber	Peru	IL	1848
● Richardson Industries	Sheboygan Falls	WI	1848
● Carter Jewelers	Jackson	MS	1849
● Hemp's Meat	Jefferson	MD	1849
● Macoy Publishing & Masonic Supply	Richmond	VA	1849
● Menasha	Neenah	WI	1849
● Nicholson & Galloway	Glen Head	NY	1849
● Tadich Grill	San Francisco	CA	1849
● Teeter's Furniture	Hawley	PA	1849
★ Matthews International	Pittsburgh	PA	1850
● Oliver Brothers	Boston	MA	1850
● Preusser Jewelers	Grand Rapids	MI	1850
● Raymond Hardware	Port Sanilac	MI	1850
● Stimson Lumber	Portland	OR	1850
● Books Inc.	San Francisco	CA	1851
● C.H.Guenther & Son	San Antonio	TX	1851
★ Corning	Corning	NY	1851
● Essex Savings Bank	Essex	CT	1851
● Hotel Leger	Mokelumne	CA	1851
★ The New York Times Company	New York	NY	1851
● Smith & Sons Funeral Homes	Columbia City	IN	1851
● Bangor Savings Bank	Bangor	ME	1852
● Bath Savings Institution	Bath	ME	1852
● Brietbach's Country Dining	Balltown	IA	1852
★ Hanover Insurance Group	Worcester	MA	1852
● Schaefer & Bierlein	Frankenmuth	MI	1852
★ Aetna	Hartford	CT	1853
● Levi Strauss & Co.	San Francisco	CA	1853

• SmithGroupJJR	Detroit	MI	1853
• Staffan Mitchell Funeral Home	Chelsea	MI	1853
• Bloch Publishing Company	Jacksonville	FL	1854
* Chicopee Bancorp	Chicopee	MA	1854
• Dierbergs Markets	Chesterfield	MO	1854
• Feigi's Interiors	Saginaw	MI	1854
• McSorley's Old Ale House	NY City	NY	1854
* Westmoreland Coal Company	Englewood	CO	1854
• Baird & Warner	Chicago	IL	1855
• Collins Companies	Portland	OR	1855
* Crane	Stamford	CT	1855
• Dollar Bank	Pittsburgh	PA	1855
• NP Dodge Company	Omaha	NE	1855
• Weitz	Des Moines	IA	1855
• Hanby Lumber Company	Berryville	AR	1856
• Orvis	Sunderland	VT	1856
• Pacific Storage Company	Stockton	CA	1856
* Barnes Group	Bristol	CT	1857
• Cooper Chemical Company	Long Valley	NJ	1857
• Northwestern Mutual	Milwaukee	WI	1857
* The McClatchy Company	Sacramento	CA	1857
* Bemis	Neenah	WI	1858
* Eastern Company	Naugatuck	CT	1858
• Gundlach Bundschu Winery	Sonoma	CA	1858
• Winglemire Furniture	Holly	MI	1858
• Graafschap Hardware	Holland	MI	1860
• Langeland-Sterenberg & Yntema Funeral Homes	Holland	MI	1860
• Wilson Bohannan Padlock Company	Marion	OH	1860
• Bassetts Ice Cream	Philadelphia	PA	1861
* Hanger Inc.	Austin	TX	1861

● Heimerdinger Cutlery	Louisville	KY	1861
● Café du Monde	New Orleans	LA	1862
★ 1st Source Corp	South Bend	IN	1863
★ Dime Community Bancshares	New York	NY	1864
★ Independent Bank Corp	Ionia	MI	1864
★ Glatfelter	York	PA	1864
★ The First Bancorp	Damariscotta	ME	1864
● American Hotel Register Company	Vernon Hills	IL	1865
● Cargill	Minnetonka	MN	1865
★ Carter's Inc.	Atlanta	GA	1865
● DWS Printing Associates	Deer Park	NY	1865
★ Hawthorn Bancshares	Jefferson City	MO	1865
● Kositchek's	Lansing	MI	1865
● Langlois Pianos	Bremerton	WA	1865
● Dickinson Brands	East Hampton	CT	1866
● Dyke Industries	Little Rock	AR	1866
● Garland Manufacturing	Saco	ME	1866
★ General Mills	Golden Valley	MN	1866
★ Huntington Bancshares	Columbus	OH	1866
● Norway Savings Bank	Norway	ME	1866
★ Sherwin-Williams	Cleveland	OH	1866
★ Acme United Corp	Fairfield	CT	1867
● Biddeford Savings Bank	Biddeford	ME	1867
● Hoekstra's Hardware	Kalamazoo	MI	1867
● Bachrach Photography	New York	NY	1868
● Benjamin Obdyke	Horsham	PA	1868
● Gorham Savings Bank	Gorham	ME	1868
★ McIlhenney Company	Avery Island	LA	1868
● Naegelin's Bakery	New Braunfels	TX	1868
★ Proctor Funeral Home Inc.	Camden	AR	1868
● Sieb Plumbing, Heating & Air Conditioning	Monroe	MI	1868

★	Campbell Soup Company	Camden	NJ	1869
●	Dime Bank	Norwich	CT	1869
★	Elmira Savings Bank	Elmira	NY	1869
★	Goldman Sachs	New York	NY	1869
●	Graybar Electric Company	St. Louis	MO	1869
●	Jelly Belly Candy Company	Fairfield	CA	1869
●	Mohonk Mountain House	New Paltz	NY	1869
●	Skowhegan Savings	Skowhegan	ME	1869
●	Androscoggin Bank	Lewiston	ME	1870
★	Brown-Forman Corporation	Louisville	KY	1870
●	DeCamp Bus Lines	Montclair	NJ	1870
●	Graeter's	Cincinnati	OH	1870
●	Star of the West Milling Company	Frankenmuth	MI	1870
★	Tennant Company	Minneapolis	MN	1870
●	White's Marble Works	Madisonville	TN	1870
★	Woodward, Inc.	Fort Collins	CO	1870
●	French Paper Company	Niles	MI	1871
●	Homer Laughlin China Company	Newell	WV	1871
●	Kennebunk Savings	Kennebunk	ME	1871
●	White Rock Beverages	Whitestone	NY	1871
●	First National Bank of Fort Smith	Fort Smith	AR	1872
●	Hammer Medical Supply	Des Moines	IA	1872
★	Kimberly-Clark	Irving	TX	1872
★	Lakeland Financial Corp	Warsaw	IN	1872
●	Maloy Risk Services	Princeton	NJ	1872
★	Ohio Valley Banc Corp.	Gallipolis	OH	1872
●	Von Maur	Davenport	IA	1872
●	Brammall Industrial Supply	Benton Harbor	MI	1873
★	Horizon Bancorp	Michigan City	IN	1873
●	Kohler Company	Kohler	WI	1873
★	Neenah Paper	Apharetta	GA	1873

● Sempliner's Bride & Formal	Bay City	MI	1873
● White Insurance Agency	Fremont	MI	1873
● D. Picking & Co.	Bucyrus	OH	1874
● Votruba Leather Goods	Traverse City	MI	1874
★ Columbus McKinnon	Amherst	NY	1875
● Daniel Orr Sons Hardware	North Branch	MI	1875
● Keep & Martinson Lumber	Tekonsha	MI	1875
● Wood, Smith, Schnipper, Clay & Vines	Hot Springs	AR	1875
● A. Schwab's	Memphis	TN	1876
● Bahle's of Suttons Bay	Suttons Bay	MI	1876
● Batesville Daily Guard	Batesville	AR	1876
● Bissell	Grand Rapids	MI	1876
● Chase Candy Co	St. Joseph	MO	1876
● Dickinson's Hardware	Fennville	MI	1876
★ Eli Lilly and Company	Indianapolis	IN	1876
● Hendrick Manufacturing	Carbondale	PA	1876
● Jockey International	Kenosha	WI	1876
★ Ladenburg Thalmann	Miami	FL	1876
● Saeman Lumber	Cross Plains	WI	1876
● Carrollton Bank	Carrollton	IL	1877
★ Greif, Inc	Delaware	OH	1877
● Patrons Oxford Insurance	Auburn	ME	1877
★ Patterson Companies	St. Paul	MN	1877
● Ebonex	Melvindale	MI	1878
● Geiger	Lewiston	ME	1878
● First Nebraska Bank	Valley	NE	1879
● Masters-LaLonde Shoes	Alpena	MI	1879
● Parker & Bailey	Walpole	MA	1879
★ Ball Corporation	Broomfield	CO	1880
● Freeport Press	Freeport	OH	1880
● Glen Raven, Inc.	Glen Raven	NC	1880

The Century Club Companies

⋆ Starrett	Athol	MA	1880
● Post Familie Vinyards	Altus	AR	1880
● Shaver Transportation Company	Portland	OR	1880
● Usinger's	Milwaukee	WI	1880
● Wiederkehr Wine Cellars	Altus	AR	1880
● Bradford White Corp	Ambler	PA	1881
● Groskopfs Luggage	Grand Rapids	MI	1881
● Seeger Metals and Plastics	Toledo	OH	1881
● Alexander Dodds Co.	Grand Rapids	MI	1882
⋆ Cabot Corporation	Boston	MA	1882
⋆ Darling Ingredients	Irving	TX	1882
● Dekker's Jewelry	Zeeland	MI	1882
● Goldens' Foundry & Machine	Columbus	GA	1882
● Ohlman Greenhouse	Toledo	OH	1882
⋆ Owens & Minor	Richmond	VA	1882
● Polar Beverages	Worcester	MA	1882
● Yale Expositor	Yale	MI	1882
● Chris Engel Greenhouse	Detroit	MI	1883
⋆ Leggett & Platt	Carthage	MO	1883
⋆ PPG Industries	Pittsburgh	PA	1883
⋆ Wolverine World Wide	Rockford	MI	1883
● Alden Shoe Company	Middleborough	MA	1884
● Garber Hardware	New York	NY	1884
● Kiewit	Omaha	NE	1884
● Seaway Printing Company	Green Bay	WI	1884
● Belden Brick Company	Canton	OH	1885
● Bemberg Iron Works	Little Rock	AR	1885
● Central Michigan Paper	Ada	MI	1885
● Clay City Pottery	Clay City	IN	1885
● Cromwell Architects Engineers	Little Rock	AR	1885
● E.C. Barton & Co.	Jonesboro	AR	1885

★ Haverty Furniture Companies	Atlanta	GA	1885
★ Johnson Controls	Milwaukee	WI	1885
● M. G. Newell	Greensboro	NC	1885
● Reusch Jewelers	Cheboygan	MI	1885
● Hayden & Sons Hardware	Cassopolis	MI	1885
● W.C. Bradley Company	Columbus	GA	1885
● First Nat'l Bank of Eastern Arkansas	Forest City	AR	1886
● American Seating	Grand Rapids	MI	1886
★ Avon Products	New York	NY	1886
● Central National-Gottesman	Purchase	NY	1886
★ Coca-Cola Company	Atlanta	GA	1886
● Gregory Insurance Agency	Piggott	AR	1886
● Hunter Fan Company	Memphis	TN	1886
● John Gallin & Son	New York	NY	1886
★ Johnson & Johnson	New Brunswick	NJ	1886
● Legacy Bank	Colwich	KS	1886
● Magnolia Metal	Omaha	NE	1886
● Mennel Milling Company	Fostoria	OH	1886
● Newberry News	Newberry	MI	1886
● S.C. Johnson & Son	Racine	WI	1886
● Sexton Pharmacy	Walnut Ridge	AR	1886
● Tipton & Hurst	Little Rock	AR	1886
● Auburn Savings Bank	Auburn	ME	1887
★ Bar Harbor Bank & Trust	Bar Harbor	ME	1887
● C.F. Sauer Company	Richmond	VA	1887
● Cummins Allison	Mount Prospect	IL	1887
● Edge-Sweets Company	Grand Rapids	MI	1887
● John Boos & Co.	Effingham	IL	1887
● Loeb's Inc.	Meridian	MS	1887
★ Malvern Bancorp	Paoli	PA	1887
● Augusta Fuel Company	Augusta	ME	1888

• Bridges Law Firm	Pine Bluff	AR	1888
• Coyle Funeral and Cremation Services	Toledo	OH	1888
⋆ Hubbell Inc.	Shelton	CT	1888
• Katz's Delicatessen	New York	NY	1888
• Kepner Scott Shoe Company	Orwigsburg	PA	1888
• Kokomo Opalescent Glass Company	Kokomo	IN	1888
• Rochester Midland Corporation	Rochester	NY	1888
• Rockland Savings Bank	Rockland	ME	1888
• Town Shop	New York	NY	1888
• Varnum	Grand Rapids	MI	1888
• AmeriPride Services	Minnetonka	MN	1889
• Bangor Publishing Company	Bangor	ME	1889
• Carhartt	Dearborn	MI	1889
• Conway Printing Company	Conway	AR	1889
• CSHQA	Boise	ID	1889
• First National Bank of North Arkansas	Berryville	AR	1889
• Goodwin Moore	Paragould	AR	1889
⋆ McCormick & Company	Sparks	MD	1889
• Modell's Sporting Goods	New York	NY	1889
⋆ MutualFirst Financial	Muncie	IN	1889
⋆ Northern Trust	Chicago	IL	1889
• Pendleton Woolen Mills	Portland	OR	1889
• Siegel Jewelers	Grand Rapids	MI	1889
• Tenenbaum Recycling Group	North Little Rock	AR	1890
⋆ A.M. Castle & Ci,	Oak Brook	IL	1890
⋆ Ameriana Bank	New Castle	IN	1890
⋆ Banner Corporation	Walla Walla	WA	1890
• Bartell Drugs	Seattle	WA	1890
⋆ Emerson Electric Co.	Ferguson	MO	1890
• First State Bank of Warren	Warren	AR	1890
⋆ Great Lakes Dredge & Dock	Oak Brook	IL	1890

★ Hardinge	Elmira	NY	1890
● Homer Monumental Works	Homer	MI	1889
● J. Levine Co. Books & Judaica	Manhattan	NY	1890
★ Lee Enterprises	Davenport	IA	1890
● Marshalltown Company	Marshalltown	IA	1890
● Oliver Products Company	Grand Rapids	MI	1890
● Pomeroy Funeral Homes	Croswell	MI	1890
★ Stifel	St. Louis	MO	1890
★ Suffolk Bancorp	Riverhead	NY	1890
● Sundt Construction	Tempe	AZ	1890
● Teufel Nursery	Hillsboro	OR	1890
● Bauer's Jewelry	Saginaw	MI	1891
● Bond Decorating	Iron Mountain	MI	1891
● Cross County Bank	Wynne	AR	1891
● First Bank of Berne	Berne	IN	1891
★ Hecla Mining Company	Coeur d'Alene	ID	1891
★ Hormel	Austin	MN	1891
● Krzyske Brothers Company	Waltz	MI	1891
★ National Bankshares	Blacksburg	VA	1891
● O'Leary Paint	Lansing	MI	1891
● Asher's Chocolates	Souderton	PA	1892
★ Bank Mutual Corporation	Milwaukee	WI	1892
● Fiorella's Sausage	Philadelphia	PA	1892
★ General Electric Company	Fairfield	CT	1892
● Johnson's Studio & Camera Shop	Cheboygan	MI	1892
● Lambrecht's Jewelers Inc.	Wilmette	IL	1892
● Mapes Furniture	Sunfield	MI	1892
● Rieck's Services	Dayton	OH	1892
● Robinson Fans Company	Zelienople	PA	1892
● Blenko Glass Company	Milton	WV	1893
★ Capitol Federal Financial	Topeka	KS	1893

• DeWitt Barrels	Marne	MI	1893
• Dittrich Furs	Detroit	MI	1893
* General Employment Enterprises	Naperville	IL	1893
• Henry the Hatter	Detroit	MI	1893
* Stewart Information Services	Houston	TX	1893
• Trimper's Rides	Ocean City	MD	1893
* West Bancorp	West Des Moines	IA	1893
• ZR Graphics	Zeeland	MI	1893
• Buckley's Shoes	Bad Axe	MI	1894
• Cowles Publishing Company	Spokane	WA	1894
• Duarte's Tavern	Pescadero	CA	1894
• Eikenhout, Inc.	Grand Rapids	MI	1894
• Frankenmuth Woolen Mill	Frankenmuth	MI	1894
• Hershey Creamery Company	Lancaster Co	PA	1894
• Hill's Sunnyside Florist	Owosso	MI	1894
• Metcalf & Jonkhoff Funeral	Grand Rapids	MI	1894
• Miner Enterprises	Geneva	IL	1894
* Hershey Company	Hershey	PA	1894
* Albany International Corp	Rochester	NH	1895
• Garland Company	Cleveland	OH	1895
• J. W. Black Lumber Company	Corning	AR	1895
• J.C. Newman Cigar Company	Tampa	FL	1895
* Kansas City Life Insurance Co	Kansas City	MO	1895
• Kirlin Company	Detroit	MI	1895
* Lennox International Inc.	Richardson	TX	1895
* Lincoln Electric	Euclid	OH	1895
• PRC Industrial Supply	Bangor	ME	1895
• Rumsey Electric Company	Conshohocken	PA	1895
• Swann's Furniture	Tyler	TX	1895
• W. W. Fairbairn & Sons	Alanson	MI	1895
• Donckers Candies & Gifts	Marquette	MI	1896

● Faultless Healthcare Linen	Kansas City	MO	1896
● Lodge Manufacturing Company	South Pittsburg	TN	1896
● Schmitt Music	Brooklyn Center	MN	1896
★ Becton Dickinson and Company	Franklin Lakes	NJ	1897
● Chelsea State Bank	Chelsea	MI	1897
★ Dow Chemical Company	Midland	MI	1897
● Glik's	Granite City	IL	1897
● Gordon Food Service	Grand Rapids	MI	1897
★ J.M. Smucker Company	Orrville	OH	1897
● Louis Maull Company	St. Louis	MO	1897
★ Middlesex Water Company	Iselin	NJ	1897
● RDK Engineers	Andover	MA	1897
★ Tootsie Roll Industries	Chicago	IL	1896
● United Pickle Products Corp	Bronx	NY	1897
● American Nickeloid Co	Peru	IL	1898
● Bank of England	England	AR	1898
● Bank of Gravett	Gravette	AR	1898
● Bechtel Corporation	San Francisco	CA	1898
● Detroit Store Fixture Company	Detroit	MI	1898
★ Goodyear Tire and Rubber Company	Akron	OH	1898
● King Koil	Willowbrook	IL	1898
● Mosher's Jewelers	Port Huron	MI	1898
● Rambusch Decorating Company	Jersey City	NJ	1898
● Vita Food Products	Chicago	IL	1898
● Warnock Furniture Co.	Magnolia	AR	1898
● Weldon, Williams & Lick	Hugo	MN	1898
● Glamos Wire Products	Fort Smith	AR	1899
★ Hooper Holmes Inc.	Olathe	KS	1899
● Seroogy's Chocolates	DePere	WI	1899
★ Sonoco Products Company	Hartsville	SC	1899
★ Timken Company	North Canton	OH	1899

The Century Club Companies

★	Wausau Paper Corp	Mosinee	WI	1899
★	Wayne Savings Bancshares	Wooster	OH	1899
●	Armstrong International	Stuart	FL	1900
●	Banner Banks	Biramwood	WI	1900
●	Block Communications	Toledo	OH	1900
●	Dykstra Funeral Home	Holland	MI	1900
●	Fris Office Outfitters	Holland	MI	1900
●	Getz's	Marquette	MI	1900
●	Gilbert Chocolates	Jackson	MI	1900
●	Graniterock	Watsonville	CA	1900
●	Lovejoy, Inc.	Downers Grove	IL	1900
●	McNerney Companies	Northwood	OH	1900
●	NEP Telephone Company	Forest City	PA	1900
●	Rosa Food Products	Philadelphia	PA	1900
●	Schramm	West Chester	PA	1900
●	French Oil Mill Machinery Company	Piqua	OH	1900
★	Weyerhaeuser Co	Federal Way	WA	1900
●	Wright Lindsey & Jennings	Little Rock	AR	1900
●	Baystate Financial	Boston	MA	1901
●	Buffalo Rock Company	Birmingham	AL	1901
●	Chelsea Milling Company	Chelsea	MI	1901
●	DeVries Jewelry	Grand Rapids	MI	1901
●	Eads Brothers Furniture Company	Fort Smith	AR	1901
★	El Paso Electric	El Paso	TX	1901
★	Harvard Bioscience	Holliston	MA	1901
●	Idaho Candy Company	Boise	ID	1901
●	Kindel Furniture Company	Grand Rapids	MI	1901
●	Kuhlman Corporation	Maumee	OH	1901
●	Michigan Ladder Company	Ypsilanti	MI	1901
★	Nordstrom	Seattle	WA	1901
●	Perfection Bakeries	Ft. Wayne	IN	1901

● Ruebel Funeral Home	Little Rock	AR	1901
● Straub's Fine Grocers	Clayton	MO	1901
● Warren Bank & Trust	Warren	AR	1901
★ 3M	Maplewood	MN	1902
★ Bassett Furniture	Bassett	VA	1902
● Crandell Funeral Home	Fremont	MI	1902
★ Fauquier Bankshares	Warrenton	VA	1902
● Fritz's Family Restaurant	Richville	MI	1902
★ G&K Services	Minnetonka	MN	1902
● Griffith Company	Brea	CA	1902
● Holland Peanut Store	Holland	MI	1902
★ J.C. Penney Company	Plano	TX	1902
● J.R Bever Company	Gentry	AR	1902
★ LB Foster	Pittsburgh	PA	1902
★ Manitowoc Company	Manitowoc	WI	1902
★ Ocean First Financial Corp	Toms River	NJ	1902
● Ott Insurance	Conway	AR	1902
● Scheels All Sports	Fargo	ND	1902
★ Stein Mart Inc.	Jacksonville	FL	1902
● Wagman, Inc.	York	PA	1902
● Washington Trust Bank	Spokane	WA	1902
● Anderson Corporation	Bayport	MN	1903
● Bodcaw Bank	Stamps	AR	1903
● DeQueen Abstract Co. Inc.	De Queen	AR	1903
● Farris Agency, Inc.	Conway	AR	1903
★ Ford Motor Company	Dearborn	MI	1903
● Geneva Worldwide	NY	NY	1903
● Herter Music Center	Bay City	MI	1903
● Jenkins Brick & Tile	Montgomery	AL	1903
● Jesperson's Restaurant	Petoskey	MI	1903
★ Simmons First National Corp.	Pine Bluff	AR	1903

• Smith Floral & Greenhouse	Lansing	MI	1903
• Triest & Sholk Inc.	Charleston	SC	1903
• Bank of Prescott	Prescott	AR	1904
• City Drug Co.	Paragould	AR	1904
• D.L. Evans Bank	Albion	ID	1904
• Hebron Brick Company	Hebron	ND	1904
• Isgro Pasticceria	Philadelphia	PA	1904
• Maneki Restaurant	Seattle	WA	1904
• Spiewak & Sons	NY	NY	1904
• Stock Yards Bancorp Inc.	Louisville	KY	1904
• Vail Rubber Works, Inc.	St. Joseph	MI	1904
★ American National Insurance Company	Galveston	TX	1905
★ Artesian Resources Corp	Newark	DE	1905
★ Badger Meter Inc.	Milwaukee	WI	1905
• Boar's Head (Brunckhorst's)	Sarasota	FL	1905
• Bulman Products Inc.	Grand Rapids	MI	1905
★ C.H.Robinson Worldwide	Eden Prairie	MN	1905
• Columbia Restaurant	Tampa	FL	1905
• The Fremont Company	Fremont	OH	1905
• G.B. Russo & Son	Grand Rapids	MI	1905
• Golden Shoes	Traverse City	MI	1905
• HEB Grocery Company	San Antonio	TX	1905
★ Herman Miller, Inc.	Zeeland	MI	1905
• Horween Leather Company	Chicago	IL	1905
• J W Hulme Company	St. Paul	MN	1905
• Louis Padnos Iron & Metal Company	Holland	MI	1905
• Lovewell Corner Store	Lupton	MI	1905
• Manson Construction Co.	Seattle	WA	1905
• Milkins Jewelers	Wyandotte	MI	1905
★ National Presto Industries	Eau Claire	WI	1905
• Red Wing Shoe Company	Red Wing	MN	1905

● Stevens Worldwide Van Lines	Saginaw	MI	1905
● Tabatchnick Fine Foods	Somerset	NJ	1905
● Ward Office Furniture	Modesto	CA	1905
● Wigwam Mills	Sheboygan	WI	1905
● Yakima Federal Savings & Loan	Yakima	WA	1905
● American Greetings	Cleveland	OH	1906
● Barbetta Restaurant	New York	NY	1906
● Conti	Edison	NJ	1906
● Democrat Printing & Lithographing	Little Rock	AR	1906
● F&M Trust	Chambersburg	PA	1906
● Fante's	Philadelphia	PA	1906
● Frankenmuth News	Frankenmuth	MI	1906
● House Hasson Hardware	Knoxville	TN	1906
★ Kellogg Company	Battle Creek	MI	1906
★ Kewaunee Scientific Corp	Statesville	NC	1906
● Leviton	Melville	NY	1906
● New Balance	Boston	MA	1906
★ Schnitzer Steel Industries	Portland	OR	1906
● Sloan Valve Company	Franklin Park	IL	1906
● United States Bakery/ Franz Bakeries	Portland	OR	1906
● Wehrenberg Theatres	St. Louis	MO	1906
★ Xerox	Norwalk	CT	1906
● Amica Mutual Insurance	Lincoln	RI	1907
● Fraunces Tavern	NY City	NY	1907
● Leupold & Stevens Inc.	Beaverton	OR	1907
★ United Parcel Service	Sandy Springs	GA	1907
● Kaap's Old World Chocolates	Green Bay	WI	1907
● Apothecary Gift Shop	Holland	MI	1908
● Armaly Brands	Walled Lake	MI	1908
● Berdine's Five and Dime	Harrisville	WV	1908
★ Briggs & Stratton	Wauwatosa	WI	1908

• Bush Brothers and Company	Knoxville	TN	1908
• C.C. Wagner & Company	Summit	IL	1908
• Chelsea Lumber Company	Chelsea	MI	1908
∗ Citizens Holding Company	Philadelphia	MS	1908
• Dennis Paper & Food Service	Bangor	ME	1908
∗ F&M Bank Corp.	Timberville	VA	1908
• Gresham State Bank	Gresham	WI	1908
• Harley Ellis Devereaux	Southfield	MI	1908
• Holler House	Milwaukee	WI	1908
• Irwin Seating Co, Inc.	Grand Rapids	MI	1908
• Pero Vegetable Company	Delray Beach	FL	1908
• Yale University Press	New Haven	CT	1908
• Cascarelli's of Albion	Albion	MI	1909
• Arthur D. Little	Boston	MA	1909
∗ Empire District Electric Co	Joplin	MO	1909
∗ Ennis Inc.	Midlothian	TX	1909
• Geiger Brothers	Jackson	OH	1909
• Munoz Photography	Fort Lauderdale	FL	1909
• Mutual of Omaha Insurance Co	Omaha	NE	1909
• P.C. Richard & Son	Farmingdale	NY	1909
• Schuler's Restaurant	Marshall	MI	1909
• Spoetzl Brewery	Shiner	TX	1909
• Superior Sports Store	Holland	MI	1909
• Tillamook County Creamery	Tillamook County	OR	1909
• Vredeveld's Shoes, Inc.	Fremont	MI	1909
• Acme Manufacturing	Auburn Hills	MI	1910
• Buis Mattress Co.	Holland	MI	1910
• Hallmark Cards, Inc.	Kansas City	MO	1910
• Ianneli's Bakery	Philadelphia	PA	1910
• Indian Trails Inc.	Owosso	MI	1910
• Koeze Company	Grand Rapids	MI	1910

● Steepleton	Lexington	KY	1910
● Esposito's Meats	Philadelphia	PA	1911
● Hathaway Dinwiddie	San Francisco	CA	1911
★ IBM	Armonk	NY	1911
● Mars Inc.	McLean	VA	1911
● P.A. Hutchinson	Scranton	PA	1911
● Skaff Furniture & Carpet	Flint	MI	1911
★ Whirlpool Corporation	Benton Harbor	MI	1911
● Wm. B. Eerdmans Publishing Co.	Grand Rapids	MI	1911
● Woolpert	Dayton	OH	1911
● L.L. Bean	Freeport	ME	1912
● Palmer Auto Service	Chelsea	MI	1912
★ Steelcase Inc.	Grand Rapids	MI	1912
● Lokker Shoes	Holland	MI	1913
● American Pop Corn Company	Sioux City	IA	1914
● Amstore	Grand Rapids	MI	1914
● Becharas Brothers Coffee	Highland Park	MI	1914
● California Casulty	San Mateo	CA	1914
● Demaco	W. Melbourne	FL	1914
● Hanover Fire & Casualy	King of Prussia	PA	1914
● Johnson Smith Company	Bradenton	FL	1914
● Mechanical Devices Company	Bloomington	IL	1914
● R.S. Lewis Funeral Home	Memphis	TN	1914
● Russ & Daughters	Manhattan	NY	1914
★ Toro	Bloomington	MN	1914
● Utility Trailer Mfg Co.	City of Industry	CA	1914
● Vogue Tyre & Rubber Co.	Mt. Prospect	IL	1914
● Baker Roofing Co.	Raleigh	NC	1915
● Bealls Inc.	Bradenton	FL	1915
● Black & Veatch	Overland Park	MO	1915
● Birnn Chocolates of VT	South Burlington	VT	1915

The Century Club Companies

∗	Commercial Metals Company	Irving	TX	1915
∗	Donaldson Company	Bloomington	MN	1915
•	Gannett Fleming	Harrisburg	PA	1915
∗	Gordman's Stores Inc.	Omaha	NE	1915
•	Haven's Candies	Portland	ME	1915
•	Hubbell, Roth & Clark	Detroit	MI	1915
•	Moe's Sports Shops	Ann Arbor	MI	1915
•	Patrick Lumber Co	Portland	OR	1915
•	Thompson Cigar	Tampa	FL	1915
•	Union Bank and Trust Co.	Monticello	AR	1915
•	Welch Allyn	Skaneateles	NY	1915
•	Western Construction Group	St. Louis	MO	1915

RESOURCES

Barney, JB. "Resource-based Theories of Competitive Advantages: A Ten-year Retrospective on the Resource-based View." *Journal of Management*, 27 (2001), 643-650.

Borzykowski, B. "America's Oldest Small Businesses." *CNNMoney* (July 30, 2013).

Collins, J. & Porras, J. *Built to Last: Successful Habits of Visionary Companies*. New York: HarperCollins Publishers, 1994.

Davis, I. "Reflections on corporate longevity." *McKinsey Quarterly* (September, 2014).

de Geus, A. *The Living Company*. Boston: Harvard Business School Press, 1997.

The Economist, "Special Report on Family Companies." (April 18, 2015), 3-15.

The Economist, "Business in the Blood." (November 1, 2014), 59-63.

Esty, D. & Winston, A. *Green to Gold: How Smart Companies Use Environmental Strategy to Innovate, Create Value, and Build Competitive Advantage*. New Haven: Yale University Press, 2006.

Fortune, "The 100 Best Companies to Work For." (March 15, 2015).

Grossman, L. & Jennings, MM. *Building a Business Through Good Times and Bad: Lessons From 15 Companies, Each With a Century of Dividends*. Westport, CT: Quorum Books, 2002.

Gunther, M. *Faith and Fortune: The Quiet Revolution to Reform American Business*. New York: Crown Business, 2004.

Hall, R. "Long Term Survivors." *Journal of General Management*, 4 (1997), 1-15.

Heugens, P., van den Bosch, F. & van Riel, C. "Stakeholder Integration: Building Mutually Enforcing Relationships." *Business and Society*, 41(1) (2002), 36-60.

Hewitt Associates. "Business Basics: People & Performance." *Hewitt Quarterly Asia Pacific*, 3 (2004).

Iwasaki, N. & Kanda, M. "Sustainability of the Japanese Old Established Companies." *Economic Institute of Seijo University*, 132 (1996), 130-160.

Kanda, M. & TenHaken, V. "A Study of Very Old Japanese Companies: Are There Common Survival Strategies?" *Global Competitiveness In a Time of Economic Uncertainty and Social Change: Current Issues and Future Expectations*, XXI (2012), 503-508.

Kwee, Z. "Investigating Three Key Principles of Sustained Strategic Renewal: A Longitudinal Study of Long-Lived Firms." *Erasmus Research Institute of Management Series in Research in Management*, 174. (2009).

Mackey, J. & Sisodia, J. *Conscious Capitalism: Liberating the Heroic Spirit of Business*. Boston : Harvard Business School Publishing, 2013.

Miller D. & Le Breton-Miller I. *Managing for the Long Run: Lessons in Competitive Advantage from Great Family Businesses*. Boston: Harvard Business School Press, 2005.

O'Hara, WT. *Centuries of Success: Lessons from the World's Most Enduring Family Businesses*. Avon, MA: Adams Media, 2004.

Ouchi, WG. *Theory Z: How American Business Can Meet the Japanese Challenge*. Boston: Addison-Wesley, 1981.

Pascale, R. *The Art of Japanese Management*. New York: Warner Books, 1982.

Pfeffer, J. *The Human Equation: Building Profits by Putting People First*. Boston: Harvard Business School Press, 1988.

Porter, M. & Kramer, M. "Creating Shared Value." *Harvard Business Review*. (January-February, 2011), 63-77.

Rosener, J. "Ways Women Lead." *Harvard Business Review*. (November-December, 1990), 119-125.

Senge PM. *The Fifth Discipline: The Art & Practice of Learning Organizations*. New York: Doubleday/Currency, 1990.

Stadler, C. *Enduring Success: What We Can Learn from the History of Outstanding Corporations*. Redwood City: Stanford University Press, 2011.